PAXTON'S PALACE

By the same author:

PAXTON'S PALACE

Anthony Bird

CASSELL · LONDON

CASSELL & COMPANY LTD

an imprint of
Cassell & Collier Macmillan Publishers Ltd
35 Red Lion Square, London WC1R 4SG
and at Sydney, Auckland, Toronto, Johannesburg

and an affiliate of The Macmillan Publishing Company Inc, New York

First published 1976

ISBN 0 304 29498 5

Printed in Great Britain by
Northumberland Press Ltd,
Gateshead
F175

Contents

Illustrations

Preface

Between 1 May and 15 October 1851 rather more than six million people visited the Great Exhibition of Art and Industry in Hyde Park, and it sometimes seems that this total is equalled, or even exceeded, by the number of words written about the Crystal Palace in which the Exhibition was staged. In addition to a flood of newspaper and magazine articles, a deluge of descriptive books, collections of engravings, odes and other ephemera poured off the presses. The removal of the Palace and its re-erection, much enlarged, at Sydenham also caused no small flurry of penmanship; but the interest naturally waned as the Crystal Palace grew unfashionable and shabby. During the first three decades of this century the Victorian era, with its personalities and its products, was generally held in small esteem, but a more sympathetic eye was beginning to be turned upon it shortly before the disastrous fire of 1936 again focused attention on the Crystal Palace.

Since that time the Exhibition and the Palace have attracted the notice of historians more than once, and the centenary, which was used to justify the Festival of Britain, inspired, amongst other material, an excellent Commemorative Album by C. H. Gibbs-Smith of the Victoria and Albert Museum. Therefore it seems necessary to apologize for offering another book on the subject, and the justification for doing so lies in the 'nuts and bolts' of the construction. Previous writers on the subject have certainly made their readers aware that the Crystal Palace was the first glass-and-iron structure of its kind, that it was of <u>unparalleled size</u> and the <u>first pre-fabricated building of 'modular' form</u>, but the <u>engineering</u> and constructional <u>details</u> are scarcely touched upon.

The object of this book is to look into these details and to probe such questions as: <u>Why were all the dimensions</u> derived from a module of 24 ft.? Why did the columns and girders take the forms they did? Where and how were the materials made, how transported and how assembled? How was the whole <u>business viewed at the time</u>?

As a necessary complement to the mundane facts the <u>characters of the principal people involved</u>, both protagonists and antagonists, are also discussed. In the last century too much credit, perhaps, was given to Prince Albert and too little to Sir Henry Cole. As the author of the design Sir Joseph Paxton was certainly appreciated in his own day, but Charles Fox, who played such a vital part in turning Paxton's dimensioned drawings into engineering reality, has been undervalued. An attempt has been made to redress these balances and to show that Henry Cole was a far-from-ordinary civil servant, just as Paxton was a most extraordinary gardener and Albert an exceptionally perspicacious Prince. The most formidable opponents of the scheme, notably Colonel Sibthorp and the King of Hanover, are also given a chance to voice their objections.

The speed with which the Crystal Palace was erected has often been remarked upon, but little attempt has been made to explain either how this was achieved, or <u>how it compares</u> with <u>modern methods</u> which would almost certainly take very much longer. One of the unpleasant facts to emerge as science and technology make ever more rapid advances is that although <u>modern man can do difficult things very</u> <u>quickly, simple things take longer and longer</u>. As the majority of mankind is, and will be, more concerned with the simple things this constitutes a growing source of injustice and frustration. By burning enough scarce petroleum to light and heat a fair-sized village for a week, a Concorde aeroplane can carry some thirty over-privileged people (who do not pay the full cost) across the Atlantic in three hours, but carrying a letter over the forty miles between Odiham and London not infrequently now requires three days—or more. That the Crystal Palace was put up in twenty-two weeks, and fitted out and painted in another sixteen, struck the world of 1851 as wonderful, and it is a sad reflection that it strikes the world of 1974 as almost incredible. From the machining of the column-joints to the paint-dipping of the glazing bars the small miracle is described in detail, and if there is a moral to be drawn from the speed of the operation the reader is left to draw it.

I would like to record my gratitude to all those named below who have helped with advice or information: Mr C. H. Gibbs-Smith of the Victoria and Albert Museum, for much helpful information; Mr Patrick Beaver for access to his remarkable collection of pictures; Mr Colin J. Ashford for a copy of his painting of the aeronautical view of the rebuilt Palace; Dr David Fisher of Freeman, Fox and Partners, successors to the original contractors; Mr Charles Allix for photocopying material about Shepherd's electric clock; the late L. T. C. Rolt for information and for permission to quote from his *Victorian Engineering*; John Murray & Co. for permission to quote from *1851 and the Crystal Palace* by Christopher Hobhouse; the Estate of Violet Markham for permission to quote from *Paxton and the Bachelor Duke*; Sir Hugh Chance for information about the family firm of Chance Brothers and Company who made the glass; Mrs Dutnall, great-great-granddaughter of Sir Henry Cole for looking into family records; and the Secretaries respectively of the Royal Commission for the Exhibition of 1851 and the Royal Society for the Encouragement of Arts, Manufacturers and Commerce for their valiant but unsuccessful attempts to find copies of the many rejected plans for an Exhibition building.

Odiham   ANTHONY BIRD
1974

1 The Idea

In 1974 as the supposedly affluent people of the industrialized countries try to come to terms with the unpalatable facts of life and realize they have been living in cloud-cuckoo land, it seems almost incredible that only 125 years ago the belief in uninterrupted and almost limitless progress was unchallenged. Even the few who saw evil in the system did not seriously doubt that material progress would continue *ad infinitum*. Nowhere was the belief stronger than in Britain where evidence of the benefits of progress was to be seen on every side. True, it could be—and often was—pointed out that the benefits were very unfairly distributed, that those who laboured in the mines, mills and manufactories to make Britain great lived lives which were in some respects even meaner and more degraded than those of the rustic poor of the previous century. To this the advocates of unfettered progress were able to point out that if more of the same drug were taken it would stop poisoning the system and begin to work a cure. Yes, they said, in effect, there is terrible poverty, with those in work paid barely enough to live on and those out of work almost wholly dependent on private charity, but an abundant supply of cheap labour means an abundant supply of manufactured goods which buys an abundant supply of cheap food without which the poor would be not only poor but dead—as they had so recently been in Ireland. Yes, the conditions of filth, disease and ignorance in which the poor lived were disgraceful, but the advancement of science and engineering would bring, amongst other things, piped sanitation and adequate supplies of pure piped water to more and more people. Better a row of back-to-back terrace houses in one of the new manufacturing towns, each with one cold tap in the kitchen and a water-closet shared in the ratio of one-to-four than a picturesque but crumbling rustic labourer's cottage with no sanitation at all and erratic water supplies from a probably contaminated well a quarter of a mile away. More manufactories might offend the eye and the nose, but if they provided cheap cotton underclothing in place of expensive linen, and cheap soap to combine with the abundant water, they would bring the cleanliness which is next to godliness; with godliness would come temperance and diligence so that the 'great unwashed' of one decade would become the 'industrious artisan' of the next, ready to make more water-pipes, more soap, more cheap clothing, coal-gas, railways, steam ships, cooking ranges, electric telegraphs and all the other wonders of Victorian technology.

It is easy enough now to poke fun at these beliefs but the founding fathers of the Industrial Revolution, men like Abram Darby, Matthew Boulton, James Watt and many more had been as much concerned to ease the lot of the labouring poor as to enrich themselves. They did have a sense of social obligation as well as technical and entrepreneurial skills, and by 1850 the belief in progress, in all its forms, did seem justified. With the possible exception of Imperial Russia, Great Britain was the richest nation in the world and certainly the most influential—and envied. Despite all the set-backs from the rick-burning and threshing machine-breaking of the 1820s to the Chartist riots and the tragedy of the Irish famine in the 1840s, political life had been tolerably stable whilst undergoing some major reforms, the internal affairs of the country ran more smoothly and the labouring poor enjoyed relatively greater prosperity than their counterparts in most Continental countries. This relative prosperity rested fairly and squarely upon material progress, and in the first half of the nineteenth century the Industrial Revolution had blighted far less of the country than had been enhanced by the less-publicized Agrarian Revolution. Despite the sulphurous slag-heaps, stinking slums, poverty, prostitution, complacency and crime Victorian progress was a god, and it was time for the god to be enshrined, at least temporarily, in a suitable temple.

Public exhibitions of arts and manufactures, of scientific and technological impedimenta, were not new, and they have become commonplace since, but three features single out the Great Exhibition of 1851 from all others. It was the first to be on a big enough scale to warrant the designation 'great'; it was the first to be international in scope, and it was the first—and last—to be financially profitable. It would have been none of these things without the Crystal Palace as the glittering temple in which both the devotees and the slaves of progress could join in worship.

Just as three features single out the Great Exhibition from others, so were three men primarily responsible for it. These were H.R.H. Prince Albert, not yet officially titled Prince Consort, Mr Henry Cole and Mr Joseph Paxton, both of whom were subsequently knighted.

Because of his position, writers of biographies and histories have been rather too ready to echo Queen Victoria's view that the idea of an international exhibition, its planning and its resounding success were, 'All, *all* the work of my beloved angel....' In his biography of the Prince, *Albert: Prince Consort*, Hector Bolitho credits Albert with having the idea of making the next Royal Society of Arts' Exhibition international in scope as early as 1849, and he is often credited with the design of the Crystal Palace itself. Perhaps the business can best be summarized by saying that without Henry Cole the Great Exhibition would never have been conceived, without the Prince it would not have been born alive and without Joseph Paxton a hostile public would have smothered the infant before it was out of its swaddling clothes.

The link that bound these three men together was that they were all fundamentally middle-class. This may seem implausible until it is remembered that the much-derided English class structure is not only remarkably flexible, but that the flexibility allows movement both ways. Henry Cole *was* the archetypal middle-class civil servant with interests and friendships ranging far beyond the scope of his official post as one of four assistant-keepers of the Public Record Office; and although he was an exceptional man it was not exceptional in Victorian England that a Joseph Paxton should rise from a humble start as gardener to the Duke of Devonshire to middle-class status, to well-deserved success, to membership of Parliament and to a knighthood. The third of the trio might be the husband of the most influential monarch in the world, and, in fact, the unacknowledged King-Regnant by the 1850s, but he was in origin the younger son of the dissolute and impoverished, mediatized, and therefore only nominally reigning, sovereign duke of a petty Thuringian duchy half the size of an average English county. Prince Albert embodied middle-class attitudes and virtues to a quite remarkable degree, and the virtues were not then despised and ridiculed as they are today. The Victorians were able to see that nearly all the men (and not a few women) who made Britain great in engineering, science, commerce and in the arts were of middle-class origin or—like Paxton—had become assimilated. The middle-class *mores* of hard work, self-help, determination, unimpeachable integrity were then actually admired, and it is very fitting that the mid-Victorian Temple of Progress was brought into being by three men whose lives were strictly governed by the middle-class code.

Local or state trade fairs were relatively common in the Germany of Prince Albert's youth, and quinquennial industrial exhibitions were held in Paris in the second quarter of the nineteenth century. In England the first such exhibition was staged by the Society of Arts as early as 1756. This Society, founded in 1753, was not so much concerned with Art, with a capital A, in the forms of pictures,

4

sculpture or music, as with the world of the artificial in its original sense of ingenious or inventive. The Society might well award a medal to the painter of an exceptionally fine picture, but was rather more likely to reward the designer of a new reaping-machine or the maker of an improved form of carriage-spring. The distinction between 'artist' and 'artisan' remained blurred until the nineteenth century was well advanced, when the former was elevated to a place of artificial (in the modern sense) superiority whilst the latter sank to the level occupied by the 'rude mechanical' of Shakespeare's day.

By the end of the eighteenth century the Society of Arts had become almost moribund, but other bodies sporadically organized trade shows or industrial exhibitions. The Royal Dublin Society, for example, started triennial shows of Irish arts, manufactures and agricultural products in 1829, and in 1845 a great Bazaar of British Manufactures was staged in Covent Garden to raise funds for the Anti-Corn-Law League. Though relatively modest this was successful, and later in the same year the Society of Arts, beginning to emerge from its torpor under the leadership of Robert Stephenson, then at the height of his fame as a railway engineer, put up the funds for an Exhibition of the Products of National Industry.

This exhibition was a failure because few manufacturers supported it, and the Society of Arts might have lapsed back into torpor had it not been for Henry Cole. Who was this Henry Cole? Had he been no more than an ordinary civil servant, struggling to keep a respectable front and a wife and family on the salary of an assistant-keeper at the Public Record Office, no more would have been heard of him and the Crystal Palace would almost certainly never have been built.

Assistant-keeper sounds rather mundane but in Mr Cole's time the office of Keeper was still a patronage 'job', and the assistants were, in fact, the departmental chiefs of a relatively new government office in the setting-up of which Cole had played a large part. The Record Office was only set up as a permanent department after 1836, after many successive

Commissions of Records had guarded and annotated the nation's state papers and historical records with degrees of efficiency and security varying from the nugatory to the non-existent. The papers themselves were stored in a great variety of odd governmental holes and corners, or, in one instance, in the damp cellar of a Commissioner's Islington villa, with almost no protection against fire, theft, damp or rats. After leaving Christ's Hospital school in 1823 Cole worked for a year as clerk to Sir Francis Palgrave, a barrister, and was then indentured to him. Palgrave was one of the Sub-Commissioners of Records who, in accordance with the practice of the time, handed over most of the duties to his clerk and confined his activity to pocketing the not inconsiderable fees. Henry Cole began campaigning for a better system of keeping the records, and the fire which destroyed the old Houses of Parliament, from which he personally directed the 'rescue' of the records of the Court of Augmentations for which he was responsible, added power to the movement towards a better system. In the next four years Cole played an important part in organizing the new office and his efforts included such matters as finding the best methods of preserving crumbling documents, labelling, indexing, cataloguing and advising on the safest methods of lighting and heating.

Three things singled Mr Cole out from his fellows. The first was a small but helpful private income, the second was an intelligent, inquiring mind, particularly in matters artistic and scientific, and the third was outstanding ability to get things done: in modern terms Mr Cole was a fixer. One of the first things he did was handsomely to augment his private income and official salary by journalistic work in which he concentrated on industrial design, or what was then known as 'art manufactures'. On the less mundane side of his abilities he was a very tolerable painter and a respected music critic. Under the pseudonym of Felix Summerly he wrote guide books, pamphlets and *catalogues raisonnés* of national and Continental art collections.

Cole also wrote, edited and published various journals,

6

including *The Journal of Design* through which he persuaded established painters and sculptors to apply their talents to the design of such domestic necessities as bread platters, cutlery, jugs, basins, candlesticks and so forth. Manufacturers were simultaneously induced to mass-produce the designers' work cheaply and well. Some of these 'Felix Summerly'-inspired designs, such as the bread platter modelled by J. Bell, have survived in production to this day; and although later generations might find some of the objects (particularly some of the electro-plated ware) too fussy, most of them are refreshingly free from the usual characteristics of the time of over-decoration, incongruity, poor proportions and wishy-washy sentimentality of the 'every-picture-tells-a-story' sort. Cole also experimented with new methods of picture-reproduction by electro-typography and other means. His best known publication, *Felix Summerly's Home Treasury* covered a wide range of interests and included the publication of children's books which, for the first time, were well illustrated by proper artists, living or dead, instead of by the usual crude hack draughtsmanship of the time. Finally, all those who benefit from the prosperity of the ever-growing greetings-card industry should raise their hats in memory of Henry Cole, because the world's first Christmas card was published by *Felix Summerly's Home Treasury* in 1846.

In 1845 the Society of Arts recognized that British technical superiority in pottery—particularly that which stemmed from the new invention of 'bone china', rivalling in delicacy and translucency the finest hard-paste porcelain but at less cost—was losing ground before French and German superiority in design and decoration. Accordingly the Society of Arts offered a prize for the best design of tea service; the prize went to 'Felix Summerly', and Henry Cole benefited greatly from the royalties paid him on the sale of thousands of sets of Felix Summerly's Tea Service made by Messrs Minton of Stoke.

Activities such as these brought Henry Cole into close acquaintance with many leading manufacturers, and he also hob-nobbed with some of the most illustrious middle-class reformers of the day. His close friends included John Stuart Mill, Chadwick the great sanitarian (who did more to improve the lot of London's poor than a whole raft of revolutionaries) and, as a fellow free-trader, Cobden of anti corn-law fame.

It is not altogether surprising therefore that after the success of Felix Summerly's Tea Service the Society of Arts asked Cole's advice about the best subjects in the Decorative Arts on which to bestow awards and scholarships from their funds. Having done this they took the logical next step of electing him to their Council and things began to move. In 1846 the Society sent a deputation, which included Mr Cole, to seek Prince Albert's support, and early in the following year the Prince accepted the office of President and procured the coveted charter which allowed the Society of Arts to call itself Royal.

Of all the many societies or institutions of which he became president or patron the interests of the Royal Society for the encouragement of Arts, Manufactures and Commerce, to use its new name, most closely matched Prince Albert's own. Of all the notable personages the Society might have chosen for its President Prince Albert was the one best suited to their needs. It was not in his nature to be merely a figurehead, and every cause he embraced was assured of tireless support, encouragement and exhortation coupled with close attention to detail and minute analysis of aims, progress and shortcomings.

In the early years of his marriage Prince Albert suffered severely because his wife allowed him no part in affairs, and he was relegated to purely decorative or social functions for which he had little liking and less aptitude. By 1845 this unhappy phase in his life was well over and he had become the Queen's unofficial principal secretary and political adviser, and, indeed, as Ministers realized, he was the uncrowned king who brilliantly completed the final transformation of the British monarchy into its modern form in which it stands above politics, cannot manoeuvre or be manoeuvred by party considerations and yet exerts considerable unseen influence on the conduct of the State.

Of all the royal persons to have earned the designation of 'the Good', Prince Albert was the one who most deserved it. He was abundantly, some might say superabundantly, good. Apart from petty jealousies over some personal relationships, and an exaggerated hatred of sexual laxity which was almost pathological, Prince Albert the Good had almost every virtue. He was handsome (as a young man, at least), intelligent, painstaking, patient, chaste, kind, far-sighted, courageous, utterly incorruptible and, alas, almost utterly unlikeable. Unlikeable to the English that is. As a German university lecturer, which he was ideally suited to be, he would have been perfectly acceptable, but as a public figure at the top of the tree in nineteenth-century England he remained alien and unacceptable. The only major mistake he made after marrying Queen Victoria was, as he put it, to remain 'a good Coburger and Gothaner'. The German princesses who had married into the English royal family since the accession of George III, such as Queen Victoria's mother or Queen Adelaide, had taken care to become thoroughly English in their manners and interests (if not always in their accents) as quickly as possible. Not so Prince Albert. He truly admired the English and a great deal of his political effort went into trying to persuade the rulers of the various foreign countries, such as Prussia, with whom he was in close contact, to adopt constitutional monarchy and parliamentary government on the English model, but he never acquired the tolerant easy-going assurance of the well-bred Englishman. He found it difficult to relax in public, and although he made jokes in private he deplored the levity and lack of seriousness apparent in so many of the leading public figures of the time. Above all he made the cardinal error of making German the private language of the English royal family. This became known and was resented. Ministers and politicians with whom he corresponded so profusely (usually via the Queen's hand and pen as part of his policy to keep her always in the forefront) could never fault the facts he arrayed in support of his arguments. Even when they disagreed with his findings they found every case well observed and cogently expressed. They admired him, they respected him, they valued his advice—but on the whole they did not like him. To all but a few intimates he seemed cold, stiff, humourless and prim and he *would* talk shop. To the masses he was and he remained a foreigner and that was enough. To the Queen he was perfection.

One of the first public appointments given to Prince Albert, on Sir Robert Peel's advice, was the Presidency of the Royal Commission to supervise the re-building of the Houses of Parliament. In this appointment the Prince had not only shown that he would never be a mere figurehead but that he was extremely well qualified to adjudicate on matters of architecture, decoration and design. He was particularly well equipped therefore to preside over the Royal Society of Arts. It was still in need of a bit of royal ginger, and because it was the very embodiment of the sort of progress he believed in the Prince could embrace its causes with genuine enthusiasm.

One of the first causes to embrace was an Exhibition of Art Manufactures held soon after the Prince became President. In characteristic phraseology he exhorted the Society that the object should be to 'wed mechanical skill with high art', and the exhibition was designed to embody the most strenuous efforts made since the days of Josiah Wedgwood to introduce both aesthetic and functional improvements into the design of every-day objects as diverse as lamps and locomotives. Princely exhortations were not enough, however, and the ultimate success of this exhibition rested entirely on Henry Cole who rescued it from failure by visiting scores of factories and making it 'a point of personal favour ... to be permitted to select from their stores a sufficient number of articles to make a show.' The resultant attendance of twenty thousand was enough to convince industrialists of the value of such shows, and they needed little persuasion to support an enlarged version of the exhibition in 1848. This attracted seventy thousand visitors despite the gloomy fears of revolution and civil disorder which were abroad in that fateful year.

The pattern was repeated in 1849 when the Royal Society of Arts staged the most important of three very successful shows in London and Birmingham. The Prince opened the highly successful Birmingham show despite discouragement from the Government who feared anti-royalist demonstrations in that most radical and chartist of cities; but everything went off well and the exhibitors were genuinely impressed with the Prince's knowledge of engineering and manufacturing problems.

Eighteen forty-nine was also the year of the eleventh quinquennial Paris Exposition which was a great success in spite of—or perhaps because of—the fact that Paris had scarcely recovered from the turmoil of kicking out the supposedly bourgeois King Louis-Philippe and replacing him with the supposedly republican Louis-Napoleon as Prince-President. In spite of his official duties, his editorships and his work of preparing a vast report on the Government Schools of Design Mr Cole found time to visit the Paris Exposition. His mind was already occupied with plans for the Society of Arts' Exhibitions for 1850 and 1851, and Prince Albert had given his blessing to the idea that 1851 should mark the start of a series of triennial exhibitions of British industry on a much bigger scale than anything hitherto attempted. With the Prince behind him Cole had persuaded the Department of Woods and Forests to grant the use of the great courtyard at Somerset House, and with considerably more difficulty, had shamed the Board of Trade into undertaking to improve upon their then half-hearted protection of copyright, the ineffectiveness of which deterred many manufacturers from putting their newest products on show.

What impressed Cole at the Paris Exposition was the technical progress the French had made since his previous visit. As far as sculpture and painting were concerned he did not greatly care for what he saw. In engineering products such as railway 'hardware', hydraulic presses, steam engines and so forth the British still had a very clear lead but in what might be called the domestic products industry French superiority was often apparent. This was particularly true, for example, in silk weaving with the invention of the Jacquard semi-automatic loom. Britain had almost no silk industry, but Cole saw that the new French processes could easily be adapted to other materials and so threaten one of Britain's principal industries. Similar considerations applied to some other exhibits and the need for an international exhibition came forcibly to Mr Cole as a result of what he saw. It was essential firstly to bring home to British industrialists the competition they had to face, and secondly to show they were not afraid to face it in a spirit of peaceful rivalry.

Far from this idea originating with Prince Albert, it was not even suggested to him until nearly a fortnight after Cole's return from Paris in mid-June. Apparently one of the first to be told was John Scott Russell, the engineer and shipbuilder, whose quarrel with his great rival, Isambard Kingdom Brunel, led to the nearly disastrous explosion of a feed-water-heater on the *Great Eastern*'s maiden voyage. Scott Russell made the principal speech at the Royal Society of Arts' distribution of prizes, in which he said there was now every hope that Prince Albert's plans for the Exhibition of 1851 could be put into effect. This brought a pretty sharp command from the Prince to attend him at Buckingham Palace to explain *what* plans he was supposed to have promulgated. Russell explained that thanks to the Prince's known enthusiasm and influence with government they had the promise of the Somerset House site and official support, hitherto conspicuously lacking. With these undertakings secured, Mr Cole had returned from Paris convinced the Society could and should put on an exhibition to outstrip the French.

Nothing was said about making the exhibition international until 27 June when Henry Cole had an interview with the Prince who recorded in the inevitable memorandum that 'The Exhibition shall be a large one embracing foreign productions and ... a Royal Commission is expedient.'

On 30 June Cole and Scott Russell again waited on the Prince, together with a Mr Fuller who was then prepared to advance £10,000 towards a prize fund. According to Mr Cole's note the Prince again stressed the 'particular advantage' which would accrue to British industry by 'placing it in fair competition with that of other nations'. Having thus neatly returned Cole's own opinion to him, the Prince went on to make the practical statement that even the huge courtyard at Somerset House would not be big enough for the scale of things they were beginning to envisage. He suggested the level site in Hyde Park opposite Knightsbridge Barracks. This seemed as harmless as it was sensible, but in the light of slightly later events the Prince might have stirred up less trouble had he proposed turning Buckingham Palace into a brothel.

2 Royal Commission and Building Committee

The Royal Commission is one of the most useful of English inventions. Like Humpty-Dumpty's use of language a Royal Commission can mean anything it chooses to mean, and it can be as sharp or as blunt, as supine or as active as circumstances require. A Royal Commission can be used to inspire or shape or suppress public feelings. It can sit for ten years discussing some trifling but inconvenient reform the government of the day knows it ought to make, but does not want to, secure in the knowledge that its recommendations, when they are made, can be conveniently pigeon-holed for another decade by which time either the need for the reform will have gone or it can be passed through Parliament without controversy. On the other hand a Royal Commission can act with startling rapidity and draconian severity secure in the knowledge that no authority can gainsay it, least of all the authority from which it derives its royal status. Like a comet, a Royal Commission has a large, flowing, ornamental tail which serves no purpose but to distract attention from the small nucleus, clustered round the paid secretary, which provides the impetus.

Prince Albert fully realized the value of a skilfully-steered Royal Commission, but six months went by before the

Government responded to his suggestion that one should be appointed, even though the draft terms of reference were written by Mr Cole and approved by the Prince the day after he had suggested the Hyde Park site. They were six very busy months for Mr Cole and a small executive committee of the Society of Arts. Long before plans for an exhibition building took shape there was much to do, and the first requirement was money. With the Prince so prominently associated with the project financial risks could not be taken, nor could the Prince afford to put up any money even if it had been proper for him to do so. The Society of Arts' funds were wholly inadequate and public, Press and Parliament in 1850 would have been aghast at the thought of using tax-payers' money for such a venture. Mr William Cubitt, the President of the Institution of Civil Engineers (not his cousin the Mr Thomas Cubitt who built Belgravia and Pimlico) estimated that a suitable building would cost £50,000; it was originally proposed to give money prizes to exhibitors and £20,000 was suggested as the least possible fund, and in all Prince Albert was not far out in his estimate that £100,000 would be needed.

The Mr Fuller who had already, with apparent disinterest, offered to launch the prize fund with £10,000 persuaded a large firm of building and engineering contractors, Messrs Munday, to agree to take all the risk in return for a propor-tion of the problematical profits from admission charges. It might have seemed a foolhardy undertaking but, making good use of the Prince's authority, Mr Cole was having such suc-cess in stumping the country wheedling promises of support from manufacturers, towns, and institutions of all kinds that it began to seem more and more likely the affair would make a profit. Even the discovery that Mr Fuller was not as disinterested as he had seemed did not discourage Mr Cole. He had contrived to get indefinite leave from the Record Office and a salary of £1,200 a year from the Society of Arts. He certainly earned every penny of it, and one of his early moves was to persuade Messrs Munday into agreeing to a clause in their contract whereby the Treasury could take over their part in the business, reimbursing them for their expenses but securing the whole profit for the country.

In between his visits to manufacturing towns in England, Scotland, Wales and Ireland Mr Cole danced attendance on Prince Albert at Buckingham Palace, Windsor, Osborne or Balmoral, being rewarded with the Prince's complete confidence and lunch or dinner at the equerries' table. Prince Albert might be the very embodiment of enlightened liberal constitutional monarchy but there was no dam' nonsense about egalitarianism. For his part, Prince Albert communicated his enthusiasm to the Government and also started the process of interesting foreign powers through his family and political connections in France, Belgium and Germany. Having swept the provincial manufacturers into his net Cole launched a massive attack on the City of London. Backed by the old East India Company, still very powerful, and with the Lord Mayor providing the Egyptian Hall at the Mansion House, a big public meeting was staged on 7 October. Charged with messages from the Prince and accounts of the support already promised, Cole won the principal city merchants and bankers to his side.

For the next stage of the business it is impossible to better Christopher Hobhouse's description in *1851 and The Crystal Palace*:

> From the time of the City meeting until the end of the year Cole's activity was prodigious. ... He paid continual visits to Windsor, where he gave Prince Albert his suggestions and received them back in the shape of commands. He danced attendance on editors and ministers. He saw the President of the Board of Trade. He sounded *The Times*. He prepared innumerable minutes for the Society of Arts. The Executive Committee held thirty-nine meetings. So complete was their success, so great their enthusiasm that many people (including Cole) began to feel that the contract with Messrs Munday was a mistake, and that the whole exhibition would be better run out of a fund provided

16

by public subscriptions than as a private speculation. The clause by which the contract remained open to revocation operated only until 1 February. The Royal Commission, foreshadowed by Prince Albert six months earlier, was therefore hastily appointed: it met for the first time on 11 January 1850, and promptly denounced the contract. The £20,000 that had been paid by Messrs Munday to the Trustees of the Prize Fund was returned and Robert Stephenson was appointed arbitrator to decide on the compensation they deserved for the loss of what was beginning to seem a very good thing; after hearing counsel on both sides, he awarded them the sum of £5,120.

History has not, alas, recorded Messrs Munday's corporate feelings but Prince Albert's Royal Commission made a good start as so much of the financial background was already prepared. However, there were only fifteen months to go to the planned opening date in which to get formal permission to use the site, to prepare it, to erect a building on it and to fill it with goodies, many from distant countries which had not yet been allocated space as nobody yet knew what space there would be to allocate to whom. It was a formidable task from which any organizing body might shrink today, but the Royal Commission at first seemed curiously unworried.

The Commission consisted of: Prince Albert, as President; Lord Granville, Vice-President; the Prime Minister, Lord John Russell; Sir Robert Peel; William Gladstone; Richard Cobden; William Cubitt (the civil engineer, not the builder) and Charles Barry the architect of the new Houses of Parliament. These constituted the nucleus and some twenty-four other gentlemen formed the ornamental tail. Most of the actual work fell on John Scott Russell and Sir Stafford Northcote (the Secretaries) and Lord Granville (the Vice-President) who was then Paymaster-General but became Foreign Secretary a little later. He was an intimate of the royal family and was Prince Albert's *alter ego* as far as the commission and its sub-committees were concerned.

The principal sub-committees—Executive, Financial and Building—were small enough to be effective. The Executive Committee, indeed, was the old Executive Committee of the Society of Arts carrying on Cole's organizational work under a new hat. The Financial Committee under Lord Granville's chairmanship managed to raise nearly £80,000 in the first ten months, after overcoming some initial resistance. This committee decided quite early to withdraw the offer of money prizes on the high-minded grounds (in which one sees Prince Albert's influence) that proficiency should be its own reward. The decision was probably right, but was understandably ill-received by potential exhibitors who found little consolation in the knowledge that Lord Macaulay and Mr Gladstone would select suitable Latin inscriptions for the medals of merit. In his capacity as vice-president of the Commission Lord Granville had little difficulty in persuading himself, in his other capacity as Foreign Secretary, to write officially to the foreign powers to solicit their co-operation.

By July 1850, with only ten months to go, it was essential to place a building contract. The difficulty that the Royal Commission, having been set up only to 'inquire into the expediency and merits of a scheme proposed by the Society of Arts' had no legal standing, was got over by the grant by the Queen of a charter of incorporation. This empowered 'our most dearly beloved consort' and his colleagues to sue and be sued, to incur and discharge liabilities and generally to behave like a commercial body. This was all very well; the Commissioners now had power to start building and their Building Committee had a plan, but the snag was that few except the authors of the building plan could view it as anything but an architectural disaster on an unprecedented scale.

By the beginning of February 1850 royal, that is, parliamentary, permission for the use of the site in Hyde Park had been given, despite some vigorous opposition, most notably from the Member for Lincoln, Colonel Charles de

Laet Waldo Sibthorp, of and from whom much more was to be heard. The Building Committee announced an open competition for would-be building designers and added the questionable proviso that if none of the plans submitted were suitable they would feel at liberty to borrow what features they liked from any or all of the rejected plans to add to a composite design of their own. Between March and May the committee received 245 plans, British and foreign, and rejected every one. Whether they were justified in doing so is not clear. No doubt many of the plans, such as that endorsed 'Lady A with great diffidence submits this plan' were too amateurish and others may have been attractive but insufficiently detailed; but a number were sent in by professional architects, builders or interior designers, like the famous Mr Crace of Wigmore Street, and it is hard to believe all these were completely worthless. Indeed, the committee reported to the Commissioners that they were 'penetrated with admiration and respect' for the valuable contributions, and they singled out sixty-eight for favourable mention and a further eighteen, twelve from French architects, for 'higher honorary distinction'.

Unfortunately, none of the 245 plans appears to have survived: the Royal Commission for the Exhibition of 1851, the Society of Arts, the Institution of Civil Engineers and the Victoria and Albert Museum have searched their shelves and cupboards in vain. The Commission's records yield no clue as to the fate of the plans once all had been rejected, yet one piece of evidence survives to indicate that they cannot have been destroyed immediately. This takes the form of a little-known book entitled *The Crystal Palace: its Architectural History and Constructional Marvels*, by Peter Berlyn and Charles Fowler junior, which formed part of the flood of ephemeral souvenirs published in 1851. Like others of its kind this little book is primarily concerned with the Crystal Palace itself and the text is little more than a re-hash of the *Official Popular Guide*, but unlike other contemporary descriptions the book does include reproductions of two of the rejected plans, one from M. Hector Horeau and the other from Messrs R. & T. Turner, also reproduced here. Interestingly enough, both buildings, like the Crystal Palace itself, are supported by iron columns and contain large glazed areas in their roofs. Both buildings appear to be inadequately supported with impossibly slender framework carrying impossibly large areas of roof, and the elaborate fussiness of M. Horeau's façade might have seemed over-done, for its purpose, even to the eyes of 1850. The Turner design is simpler externally and the interior transverse view seems gracefully attractive, but such large areas of curved iron roof with flat skylights on the scale suggested would have needed a more robust skeleton than the drawing shows.

On the grounds of cost alone both of these designs were impracticable, and M. Horeau's would have been particularly expensive as his description refers to the façade being of gilded metal, porcelain tiles and stained glass. The roof lights were to be of ground or etched patterned glass, internal doors and fittings were to be gilded or silvered, the spandrels of the roof-trusses were to be of gilded copper and there were to be lavish ornamental figures and panels in mosaic, terra-cotta, coloured glass and porcelain.

In addition to being 'penetrated with respect' for the flood of ideas it is hard to resist the conclusion that the members of the Building Committee were even more penetrated with respect for the superiority of their own talents. For the committee included such distinguished architects and engineers as Charles Barry, William Cubitt, C. R. Cockerell, Robert Stephenson and Isambard Brunel. If this formidable array of talent were not enough the Executive Committee was headed by Lt-Col. Reid of the Royal Engineers, an authority on large structures, and besides John Scott Russell the main body of Commissioners included Sir Charles East-lake, President of the Royal Academy and Sir Richard Westmacott. There was also the Prince himself whose architectural pretensions are not to be despised, even if Osborne House, in the design of which he played a large part, may not be to our taste.

Having rejected the 245 offerings the committee produced

their own plan for a building and expatiated on its merits in their report to the Commissioners who promptly accepted it; very largely, it may be supposed, because time was so short and here at least was a detailed plan with the materials and quantities specified. This official design would prompt one to remember the theory that a camel represents the attempts of a committee to design a horse, were it not for the fact that although the Building Committee took joint responsibility, the plan was very largely the work of one man. That man was Brunel and the plan seems fully to illustrate the proposition that the bigger the man the bigger the mistake.

Isambard Kingdom Brunel, the famous son of a famous father, was certainly the biggest fish in the engineering sea in 1850. He was then forty-four years old, only nine years away from his premature death, and an acknowledged master of the new age of iron and steam. His railways, particularly his Great Western, his bridges, his docks, his ships were all conceived and executed on the grandest scale. Like all great engineers he had the eye of an artist. His bridges and buildings were not only technically daring but outstandingly handsome, and his most successful ship, the *Great Britain*, was not only the first ocean-going iron ship propelled by a screw but has survived to demonstrate why connoisseurs regard her as the most beautiful steam-ship ever built. It is true that Brunel could make mistakes, often by being too far ahead of his time. Though technically correct his seven-foot gauge Great Western Railway was ultimately proved to be commercially wrong because too much track had already been laid to the old coal-cart width of 4ft. 8½in., and his forty miles of atmospheric railway in south Devon lost his shareholders a great deal of money. In 1850 Brunel's biggest venture, the *Great Eastern*, was only in the stages of initial planning. Because of her commercial failure—for which Brunel cannot be blamed—she too has been dubbed a grandiose mistake, but this is unjust, for the *Great Eastern* was a technical triumph. Five times larger than any ship previously attempted she was as easily manoeuvred as a rowing boat and she was also one of the safest ships yet built. She withstood an explosion which would have sunk any of her contemporaries, and when she touched an uncharted pinnacle of rock off Montauk Point she ripped a gash in her bottom far bigger than that which sank the unsinkable *Titanic*, without suffering more than a slight list to starboard.

All in all therefore Brunel seemed the right man to produce the right building in which to house the spirit of progress. What he did produce was a plan for a vast, squat, brick warehouse four times the length and twice the width of St Paul's Cathedral. This was to be adorned with a monstrous iron dome, which, even though it was bigger than that of the cathedral, would have looked like no more than a bowler hat on a billiard table on that vast acreage of planned roof. Christopher Hobhouse sums up this accepted plan :

> The building resembled nothing so much as an early nineteenth-century colonial Government House, all roof and veranda, entered by means of colossal false arches of horrible proportions. Perched upon this squat and monotonous shed, which was to be only sixty feet high, was a dome a hundred and fifty feet high and two hundred feet in diameter. This dome, the cherished masterpiece of Brunel, was to be made of sheet iron. Of all the wonders of industry on view, it was thought that none would be more wonderful. But it was certain that none could be more hideous.

Worse, if possible, than the building's aesthetic shortcomings was its lack of fitness for its purpose. There were, in effect, nine months in which to put it up, decorate and fill it, yet it was estimated to need at least sixteen million bricks and even if it had been possible to lay that number sufficiently quickly (to say nothing of preparing the foundations of so massive a structure) it is doubtful whether the country's brick industry could have supplied them in time.*

Opposition to the Exhibition fell under three heads: firstly there was the vociferous anti free-trade lobby, headed by Colonel Sibthorp; these were followed shortly by the doom-mongers, also led by the good Colonel, who prophesied disease, moral pollution, riot and revolution brought by the foreign riff-raff who would flood into Britain. Thirdly there were the radicals who opposed the use of the park on the firm ground that it constituted an infringement of established liberties. Though his worst enemies could not call Colonel Sibthorp a radical he was also prominent on this band-wagon. Those who opposed the use of the park had the best case which was met by promises, reiterated again and again by the Commissioners and the Government, that all traces of the exhibition would be swept away within six months of the closing date. It did not need an expert eye to see that even if the building could be put up in nine months, it would be impossible to dismantle and remove it in six, and the expense of the job—the materials would have almost no break-up value—would tempt any Government into break-ing its promise.

Another serious objection which was not widely ventilated was—ventilation. The drawings of the official design show that the wide verandas would have prevented natural light from penetrating far inside, and that only about one-eighth of the vast roof was to be sky-lit. The interior would have been interlaced with load-bearing party walls and arches so that it would have been as dark as the inside of the pro-verbial cow. Nobody appears to have calculated how many thousands of gas-jets would have been needed to light the place, but without the most elaborate system of forced draught through that monstrous dome the heat and fumes would have been intolerable.

The publication of the building Committee's plan in *The Illustrated London News* on 22 June 1850 bound the differ-

* During the building of the L. & N.W.R. Company's Euston terminus twenty million bricks were laid in about ten months, but this was achieved by drawing on unusually extensive stocks.

ent strands of opposition together and greatly strengthened
them. The first broadside had, indeed, been fired by Colonel
Sibthorp appropriately enough on Waterloo Day (18 June),
when he used Question Time in the House of Commons to
ask with apparent innocence on whose authority a clump of
ten young elm trees was marked for felling on the exhibition
site. These 'Sibthorp elms' became the rallying standard in
the battle which then began to rage, with the Colonel leading the troops and firing gun after gun from his well-stocked
armoury. Secret societies to assassinate the Queen; invasions
of papists with the consequent disasters of idolatry;
venereal disease and bubonic plague; shifty, bewhiskered
aliens hiring Kensington houses for use as brothels—all and
many more bogeys were marshalled in support of the
Colonel's cry that Hyde Park would become a ploughed field,
a rubbish dump, an armed camp, with not a tree left standing
on all four thousand acres; that the Serpentine would become
an open sewer, property prices decimated, landed pro-
prietors beggared, the constitution overthrown. . . .

These and myriads of other bogeys were deployed by
the Colonel whose real bogeyman was progress, summed up
in his dictum, uttered during discussion of a Railway Bill,
'I would rather meet a highwayman, or see a burglar on
my premises, than an engineer.' Although in 1974 one may
feel sneaking sympathy with Colonel Sibthorp, his outbursts
in 1850 might have seemed no more than comically ridiculous had they not commanded a surprising amount of
support, more temperately expressed and therefore more
effective. Not that all the opposition was less intemperate
for two former Lord Chancellors, Lord Brougham and Lord
Lyndhurst, joined the verbal fray with a degree of vehemence
which fully matched Colonel Sibthorp's.

The Times newspaper which had originally praised the
choice of Hyde Park now traversed its guns through 180
degrees in order to support the Sibthorp artillery. This was
a much more serious matter and the first salvo on 25 June
found the range at once:

The whole of Hyde Park and, we will venture to predict, the whole of Kensington Gardens, will be turned into a bivouac of all the vagabonds of London so long as the Exhibition shall continue ... The annoyance inflicted on the neighbourhood will be indescribable.

This was followed by the full barrage two days later when *The Times* had had time to digest the full horror of the proposed building, and the following passage raised echoes of support on all sides:

We are not to have a 'booth', nor a mere timber shed, but a solid, substantial edifice of brick, and iron, and stone, calculated to endure the wear and tear of the next hundred years. In fact, a building is about to be erected in Hyde Park to the full as substantial as Buckingham Palace; ... not only is a vast pile of masonry to be heaped up in the park, but one feature of the plan is, that there shall be a dome of 200 feet in diameter—considerably larger than the dome of St Paul's.... By the stroke of a pen our pleasant Park— nearly the only spot where Londoners can get a breath of fresh air—is to be turned into something between Wolverhampton and Greenwich Fair. The project looks so like insanity that, even with the evidence we have before us, we can scarcely bring ourselves to believe that the advisers of the Prince have dared to connect his name with such an outrage to the feelings and wishes of the inhabitants of the metropolis. Can anyone be weak enough to suppose that a building erected on such a scale will ever be removed? Under one pretext or another it will always remain a fixture.... The first and the main reason why we protest against the erection of this huge structure on such a site is that it is equivalent to permanent mutilation of Hyde Park. Once again we entreat the Prince and his advisers to pause ere it be too late.

The Commission and the Government put up a stout defence, but were dreading the outcome of a debate on a motion put down by Colonel Sibthorp calling on the Government to appoint a Select Committee to reinvestigate the whole scheme of the Exhibition. Had this motion been carried it would have been tantamount to a vote of no confidence, equally humiliating to the Government, the Commission and the Prince, and it would almost certainly have led to the abandonment of the project. The debate was to be held on 4 July and as an added blow the defence lost its best speaker on the 2nd when Sir Robert Peel died. Salt was rubbed into the wound because he died from injuries sustained when he fell from his horse riding home after a special meeting of the Royal Commission itself. The Prince wrote despairingly to his brother as soon as he heard of Peel's death:

> Now our Exhibition is to be driven from London; the Patrons who are afraid, the Radicals who want to show their power over the crown property, *The Times* whose solicitor bought a house near Hyde Park, are abusing and insulting. This evening a decision is to be made. Peel, who had undertaken the defence, is no more, so we shall probably be defeated and have to give up the whole Exhibition. You see we do not lie on a bed of roses.

Nor was the opposition only home grown, and the focal point abroad was the near-blind, octogenarian King Ernest Augustus of Hanover, the Queen's eldest uncle, male head of the English royal family, the last surviving son of King George III and a rabid opponent of the House of Coburg in general and Prince Albert in particular.

This 'Lord of Misrule', as Albert called him, was better known in England as the High Tory Duke of Cumberland who had qualified for the title of the best-hated man in the country for many years. He was popularly believed guilty of rape, sodomy, murder and incest as well as of plotting the assassination of the young Princess Victoria who (as the daughter of his deceased elder brother Edward) stood between him and the English throne. None of the lurid accusations were true and the Duke's real crime was that he led the extreme Tory opposition in the House of Lords in so effective, vigorous and forthright a manner as to earn the wrath and dislike of all who disagreed with him. His sarcastic tongue and sardonic humour earned him many enemies outside politics as well, and when he became King of Hanover in 1837 (female succession to the Hanoverian throne being barred whilst any male heirs survived) his enemies expected that his supposedly despotic tendencies would lead to his speedy dethronement and humiliating return to England. To their chagrin he turned out to be a surprisingly liberal, though autocratic, and hard-working ruler who earned first the respect and then the affection of his subjects. He often spoke up for the smaller states in the Federal Diet, fell foul of Prince Albert by opposing German unity under Prussian domination and founded the *Steuerverein* or taxation union of the maritime states in opposition to the Prussian *Zollverein*. Whether Prince Albert liked it or not 'old king', as his fellow sovereigns called him, wielded a good deal of influence in the protectionist northern states, and he busied himself with writing innumerable letters of inordinate length to his fellow rulers beside which Colonel Sibthorp's diatribes seemed positively benign.

In the event Colonel Sibthorp's motion was defeated, but opposition in the press grew ever fiercer and the Commissioners knew in their hearts that whilst they loyally supported the official building plan the country would not support them.

3 Joseph Paxton

If Joseph Paxton had not existed it would have been necessary for Samuel Smiles to invent him. Unfortunately the qualities of self-help, thrift, industry and morality which Samuel Smiles extolled in his *Lives of the Engineers* and other works have been at a discount for so long now that late twentieth-century eyes find it difficult to focus clearly on the sorts of self-made men the Victorians admired. Self-made men of the parvenu, speculating entrepreneur sort, who are now acceptable, were anathema to our great-grand-fathers but the working-class boy who made good in the solid productive industries was a hero, and it is notable that a large proportion of those who transformed Great Britain into a great industrial power between 1760 and 1860 were men who would have almost no chance to show their mettle in these more enlightened times. Would George Stephenson, who was almost illiterate, be hired today as surveyor, engineer, locomotive designer and general miracle worker by the Manchester and Liverpool Railway Company? Would Joseph Paxton, who had no formal qualifications as engineer and architect, be allowed a chance to design a building which was not only more than twice the size of St Paul's Cathedral but was built on principles which were virtually untested?

Joseph Paxton was a farmer's son, born in 1803,* and given little education beyond a nodding acquaintance with the three R's. In 1823 he found work as one of the gardeners at the Royal Horticultural Society's grounds which bordered the Duke of Devonshire's estate at Chiswick House. The Duke was a keen gardener and when in residence at Chiswick he used to like to stroll across to the Society's gardens to see what was going on and to pick the brains of the men who worked there. He found so much to pick in Paxton that in 1826 he took him off to be head gardener at Chatsworth.

This may have caused some jealousy in the established Chatsworth hierarchy, but the Duke's choice was soon seen to be justified as the young Paxton showed himself able to outdo Capability Brown. The lovely pleasure grounds of the great Derbyshire estate took on a new loveliness as Paxton almost literally moved mountains. At least, he diverted streams, dug lakes, lowered hills, raised valleys and moved fully-grown trees so huge that modern contractors with all their mechanical aids would flinch from the task.

Nor were all Paxton's works strictly horticultural although much of his time was spent investigating and testing new species and rare trees and shrubs which he had brought to Chatsworth from all over the world. Chatsworth was already famous for its water gardens fed from the classical cascade house built into the side of a hill; Paxton's improving hand was turned to the fountains and water displays, and in honour of a proposed visit by the Tsar Nicholas I, which never materialized, he engineered a new fountain which throws its great jet to a height of 267 feet. This is still the highest gravitational fountain in existence.

To meet the duke's wish to improve the prospect from the great house Paxton removed a complete hamlet, occupied by estate workers, and rebuilt the village and its church. This, the new model village of Edensor, was out of sight of the house itself. With the addition of electricity and other

* Some sources give the year of Paxton's birth as 1801, not 1803, but the majority seems to favour the latter.

modern niceties Edensor is still a model of what a good housing estate should be.

To house the tender species of rare plants Paxton built orchid houses, a pinetum, an arboretum and his Great Conservatory, an acre in extent with a carriage drive running through it, which the early Victorians considered one of the wonders of the age.

The Great Conservatory was remarkable chiefly for its size, but twelve years later, in 1849, Paxton followed it with a smaller, more elegant glasshouse specially designed for a special purpose. This was the famous lily house built for the giant water lily from British Guiana, discovered in Queen Victoria's accession year and named *Victoria regia* in her honour. In 1846 the Royal Botanical Gardens at Kew managed to germinate some seeds, but the plants made little growth and did not flower. Paxton contrived to procure a plant for Chatsworth and grew it in a large heated tank in which the water was kept in constant gentle motion by machinery of his design. In three months' time he was rewarded with leaves five to six feet in diameter surrounding flower buds the size of footballs.

The great leaves were strong enough to support Paxton's five-year-old daughter, and to the greatest practicable extent he copied the arrangement of radial ribs, strengthened by very slender cross ribs always in tension, in constructing the lily house to shelter the gargantuan *Victoria regia*. Lacy, delicate cast-iron work matched the delicacy of the leaf skeleton, and the roof glasses were supported on slender hollowed-out beams which also served as gutters to carry rain water into the slender cast-iron columns which supported them. Supporting columns like this had been used for drainage before, but the great lily house's combination of real strength with apparent fragility was quite new.

It is easy enough to say that Paxton could do all he did because he was backed by limitless money for ducal extravagances, but by the time the lily house was built he was far more than a mere head gardener or estate agent. Most of the ducal extravagance went on solid, useful improvements to the estates, farms and workers' houses, but in one way and another the Duke's large revenues were in a poor way by the mid-1830s and Paxton became responsible for the financial management of the external affairs of the estates at Chatsworth, Chiswick, Bolton Abbey, Hardwick and Lismore. In addition to glasshouses and pleasure gardens Paxton now became responsible for designing estate houses, farm buildings, reservoirs, bridges and gasworks. He also accompanied the duke on his foreign travels and handled the monetary side of augmenting the collections of paintings, statuary and antiques which adorned the great houses.

In the course of all these duties he became as near to being a personal friend as the customs and etiquette of the time allowed. That is, duke and former gardener relied on one another, learnt from one another, respected and liked one another but preserved the degree of public formality then thought proper between aristocrat and man of affairs. As the sixth Duke of Devonshire was a bachelor the twentieth century would inevitably see homosexuality in the relationship, but although the Victorians were ready enough to see immodesty in a female ankle and virtue in danger if a young woman ventured into a hansom cab with any man other than her husband they were able to accept that friendships between men could be no more than friendships.

Joseph Paxton grew money as successfully as he grew flowers or trees, and in the process of restoring the Duke's fortune he made his own. Through his management of his patron's extensive railway interests he was invited to sit on the boards of railway companies and other businesses. Like Mr Cole a great deal of his prosperity rested on publishing and editorial work. In association with Harrison and Lindley he published the *Horticultural Register, Paxton's Flower Garden, A Botanical Pocket Dictionary, A Practical Treatise on the Cultivation of the Dahlia, The Magazine of Botany* and a *Calendar of Gardening Operations* which has only recently been superseded. In 1846 Paxton embarked on a more ambitious project and founded the *Daily News* which survived the disastrous editorship of Charles Dickens, and the even more calamitous management of John Dickens who was not only the novelist's father but the prototype Mr Micawber, to blossom into prosperity under Charles Dilke, father of the Charles Dilke who entranced Queen Victoria when he sat upon her lap and tried to clutch her ear-rings and infuriated her when he grew up to be a republican.

Paxton's involvement with the Great Exhibition was fortuitous and happened very late in the day. Moving in railway and industrial circles as he did, and numbering such men as Robert Stephenson among his friends, Joseph Paxton doubtless heard the inside gossip about the Commission's uneasiness over the building even before the plans were published. Although he did not become a Member until a little later, Paxton also had a foot in the parliamentary camp and it was indirectly through Parliament that he became involved. This was on 11 June when he had business to discuss with Mr Ellis, M.P., who was Chairman of the Midland Railway Company.

The meeting took place in the House of Commons, and after their discussion Ellis invited Paxton to accompany him to the new debating chamber in which the house was sitting for the very first time, experimentally, to test the acoustics. The rebuilding of the Palace of Westminster after the fire in 1834 ranks with the Ecclesiastical Titles Bill, the Married Women's Property Bill and the Deceased Wife's Sister's Bill as a source of controversy, private and public squabbles, press campaigns, furious letters to *The Times*, writs and legal actions. To those who are acquainted with grandiose governmental projects in this century, such as that aeronautical white elephant the Concorde, it will occasion no surprise that the job took three times as long and cost six times as much as was estimated. The result is outwardly splendid and inwardly inconvenient, and during the long gestation and birth the principal architect, Charles Barry, was almost constantly at loggerheads with the lesser luminaries. In fairness it must be said they were often as intransigent as he. There were furious rows with, for example, Edward Beckett Dennison (later Lord Grimthorpe) who designed the movement for the great clock, which culminated almost literally in an impasse when it was discovered that there was insufficient clearance in the clock tower to hoist the hour bell, Big Ben, into place and then that the minute hands Barry designed, against Dennison's advice, were too heavy for the clock to drive. Augustus Welby Pugin carried on his work of designing the details of the Gothic ornamentation in a state of seething hatred for Barry, and all communication between them had to be by intermediaries; and Dr Reed, who designed the abysmally ineffective ventilating system, blamed its expensive failure on Barry's lateness in providing detailed drawings of the air shafts: Barry retaliated by issuing a writ for defamation of character.

It was in this happy state of affairs that Paxton and Ellis attended the trial run in the Chamber which proved that in addition to the ventilating system failing to dispel the legislative hot-air, the acoustics obliged the legislators to pit their eloquence against a cloud of cotton wool. After the session Mr Ellis spoke of the extraordinary succession of blunders which had dogged the work, and this brought from Paxton the rejoinder that if all he heard was true an even bigger blunder was about to be made over the design of the exhibition building. He added that he had some ideas of his own which he would gladly put before the Commission if they were not already too late.

This conversation took place a fortnight before the official plan was published, but it is safe to assume that Ellis, like Paxton, had his ear to the ground and realized how unsuitable the building was likely to be. Although it was late on a Friday afternoon he whisked Paxton away in a cab to the Board of Trade where he happened to know that Henry Cole would be found. Cole also welcomed the possibility of an alternative, and told his visitors that the specifications for contractors' tenders would also be issued in a fortnight, but that he thought he could persuade the Commissioners to have a clause introduced to allow an alternative plan to be submitted with a tender.

Paxton did not have even a fortnight to work at his plan,

because of engagements in Wales and Derby which he could not cancel, but he promised Mr Cole that if the suggested clause could be written into the invitations to tender he would produce finished drawings in nine days. Cole was no stranger to hard work but he was astonished by this bold undertaking. Unfortunately Cole's notes and memoirs do not reveal whether he was given any idea at this stage of the sort of building Paxton had in mind, but he knew Paxton and knew his reputation for getting things done.

According to Miss Violet Markham, Paxton's grand-daughter and biographer (*Paxton and the Bachelor Duke*), it was not until the following Tuesday that Paxton was able to put pen to paper : and then it was to blotting paper for the first sketch of the Crystal Palace was 'doodled' whilst Paxton presided over a meeting of the Midland Railway Company's disciplinary committee at Derby. This famous piece of pink blotting paper is preserved in the South Kensington Museum. Amongst scribbles and numerals relating to railway business it shows an elevation and a cross-section, which do not accurately correspond, of a large iron-framed glass building, with round-headed glass bays in groups of five, stepped up in smaller tiers like a ziggurat to a three-tier-high central nave with an internal semi-circular vault. Frilly parapets surround the flat roofs and the cross-section shows internal galleries very similar to those in the finished building.

On his return from the railway committee meeting Paxton began to transform his blotting-paper doodle into a full set of large-scale detailed plans. All this was done in seven days (and nights) of intensive work, in the small estate office at Chatsworth using the normal small staff. Most of the actual draughtsmanship appears to have been done by Paxton himself, and the only outside help came from Robert Barlow, one of the Midland Railway Company's engineers, who gave some advice about stresses in iron girders. It was an astonishing week's work. Admittedly the building plan is essentially simple, particularly in its original form, and based upon the repetition of equally-shaped and -sized components at regular

34

intervals. In modern jargon it would be called 'modular', but it has the advantage over modern modular structures, which are generally metric, that the principal module of twenty-four feet is divisible by three. Smaller units therefore went into feet and inches without awkward fractions, with the exception that ten inches was specified as the width for the panes of glass. This is not as illogical as it seems as allowance had to be made for the width of the framing and the narrow vertical glazing bars, so that twenty-eight 10 in. panes filled a 24 ft. space without cutting or wastage.

On 22 June the nine days were over and Paxton set off for London with his nine-days' wonder in the form of a large bundle of plans. From Rowsley (the station which Paxton had been instrumental in having built to serve the Chatsworth estate) he had to go to Derby to change on to the London line. Whilst waiting he encountered Robert Stephenson also waiting for the London train, and asked him to share a compartment. Stephenson was Paxton's exact contemporary, who came from an equally humble background and was at that time near the height of his success as *the* great railway builder and magnate in a railway-worshipping age. Paxton naturally knew that Stephenson was one of the Exhibition Commissioners and on the Building Committee, but when he began to talk about his plan Stephenson's immediate reaction, as he did not know of Cole's escape clause, was to say the matter was settled and that nothing could be done. As he examined the drawings however he caught Paxton's enthusiasm and promised to support him.

The next move, after reaching London, was shrewd. Instead of going straight to Cole or the Royal Commission, Paxton paid a call on Lord Brougham. Brougham had been a spent force politically for more than a decade, but he was still a popular figure able to command Press support. As he saw the plans and discussed them 'Old Wickedshifts' did as so many were to do and executed a smart about-face. It may well be that he was glad of an opportunity to rid himself of his strange bedfellows in opposition, Colonel Sibthorp and his bitterest political opponent of former times the King of

Hanover; but whatever the reason, from that moment Lord Brougham was as fervent in support of the Exhibition as he had formerly been vehement against it.

It was too much to hope that the Royal Commission and more particularly the Building Committee, would accept Paxton's gargantuan glass house without demur. From the day of his arrival in London nearly six weeks' manoeuvring, politicking, cajoling and arguing went by before final acceptance was made on 26 July. In his favour Paxton had the support of Stephenson and Cole, followed by Lord Granville and the Prince, whom he saw three days after his interview with Brougham. By this time Prince Albert was being indirectly but persistently attacked in the Press over the Exhibition, so his support was not of great value publicly however comforting it may have been privately. Of Lord Granville's support, Paxton's opponents were quick to point out that as he was the Duke of Devonshire's nephew this was simply and literally a matter of nepotism : that this objection was as unjust as it was irrelevant mattered not at all to those who raised it.

Also in Paxton's favour were the obvious ugliness and unsuitability of the official design, and Christopher Hobhouse makes the point that:

> ... at this moment, when the last remnants of his English popularity looked like being buried beneath the Committee's monstrous brick building, the Prince would have listened to almost any alternative suggestion. If Paxton had come forward with a design for an exhibition building of cardboard he would have found an attentive listener in Prince Albert.

This is true enough but overlooks an important point. Because the Prince was not personally responsible for the official design he could support Paxton without undue loss of face; but the Building Committee could not, and the preservation of face provides a powerful motive for sticking to a decision however wrong-headed it may be. Also, except for the sheet-iron dome, the official building was conventional, and if some contractor could be found who was crazy enough to undertake to provide and lay fifteen million bricks in six months (thus leaving four months to finish the interior and arrange the exhibits) then at least everybody would know what they were doing; but Paxton's great walls and roofs of iron-framed glass, eighteen *acres* covered by a glass case, were crazy—flying in the face of providence.

Of the experts on the Building Committee Barry could be relied upon to oppose anything about which he had not been consulted, and Cockerell also resented anything which came from outside the sacred ranks of professional men. Sir William Cubitt was elderly and represented the conservative views of the Institution of Civil Engineers which was just sufficiently far removed in time from its vigorous infancy under Thomas Telford to be growing suspicious of innovations. Stephenson was in favour, but Brunel, as the true father of the official abortion, could not be expected to approve. However, besides being a genius he was a truly great and generous man as the help he later gave Paxton amply proved. At one stage in the negotiations the committee asked Paxton what he could do about the few elm trees on the site. With his experience of moving mature trees Paxton would have preferred to remove and replace them, but knowing the trouble the Commission had already suffered over the smaller 'Sibthorp elms' he undertook to cover them over inside the building.

The Paxton plan was put before a special meeting of the Commissioners on 25 June (it was after this meeting that Sir Robert Peel had the fall which led to his death a week later), and reading between the lines it seems they were collectively inclined to favour the unorthodox building, but prudence and protocol required them to refer the matter to the Building Committee for full and urgent investigation.

Lord Granville was not the only man on the Commission who knew about Paxton's glass buildings and his flair for getting things done. The Prince also knew, and he had been particularly impressed by the organization of a great entertainment and *fête* in the Queen's honour, at Chatsworth, in 1843. A night-time spectacle of unprecedented brilliance had been arranged with the gardens, conservatory, trees, shrubs, statuary, fountains, cascades and pools lit up by thousands of fairy lights, reflector-lanterns, gas-flares and every resource available in the pre-electric age. The effect was magical, and the Queen and Prince were not the only ones to be astounded and to wonder how it had been managed. The Duke of Wellington was there and he not only wanted to know how it was done but how it was to be undone. To this end he rose early on the following morning only to find that not so much as a candle-end or a scorched spray of leaves was to be seen; the grass which had been charred or trampled by hundreds of feet had been dug up and returfed; the lawns had been swept and the edges re-trimmed, and all the gravelled walks newly raked and rolled. Paxton had deployed a large force of extra workmen, each given a specific task, and they had spring-cleaned several acres, by lamplight, between midnight and dawn. 'I would have liked that man of yours for one of my generals' said Wellington to Devonshire, and no greater compliment could have been paid.

The phrase 'It would never do for the Duke' was still of some significance in 1850, and applied to anything proposed in Hyde Park of which Wellington had recently been made Ranger. As always he took very seriously the duties of an office which most would have regarded as a sinecure, with the duties to be performed by a deputy whilst the fees were pocketed by the holder. This was not the Duke's way and he made himself acquainted with every detail of park maintenance and administration. Therefore the knowledge that Paxton's building would 'do for the Duke' helped allay doubts later on; particularly over the question of getting the huge structure put up in time. On this score he merely said in his terse way: 'Of course it will—Paxton says it will.'

What was ultimately good enough for the Duke was not at first good enough for the Building Committee. Quite apart from personal feelings, hurt pride and loss of face the members were on the horns of a dilemma. If they insisted on their own design they would have a 'safe' building of known characteristics, even if the exhibition staged in it would almost certainly be a failure. In adopting Paxton's building they would gamble on triumphal success or total disaster. Could such a structure of such a size have enough lateral stability? Would it be safe to house many thousands of people daily? Could it stand the weather even if it stood up? 'Everybody knew' that conservatories always leaked like a sieve and dripped with condensation, and how could manufacturers and foreign powers be expected to send precious goods to be shown where they might be ruined by rainwater?

Just as Cole's clause allowing an alternative plan to be submitted got the committee off the hook of having no alternative but to put up a building everybody disliked, so Paxton now relieved them of the odium of choosing between a safe failure and a gamble. He went over their heads and persuaded the *Illustrated London News*, which then had a circulation not far short of a quarter million, to publish an engraving of his design together with a concise explanation of its merits, which included pointing out that the building could be quickly and cheaply dismantled either to yield quantities of valuable scrap or to be re-erected elsewhere.

The date was 6 July, and it took another three weeks of discussion and argument before the committee accepted the plan, but public enthusiasm for it made it clear that they had no real alternative left but to take a chance on this 'Crystal Palace'. *Punch* clinched the matter a few weeks later when Douglas Jerrold, a pioneer staff member and a friend of Paxton's, coined this felicitous title. The Crystal Palace: the name had a magic ring to it which transformed Prince Albert's sober, serious, improving, moralizing exhibition, smothered in a brick coffin and sinking under an elephantine dome, into something which might be fun.

4 Fox, Henderson and Chance

There was much to do between the carefully planned 'leak' to the *Illustrated London News* and the Building Committee's capitulation. Whatever the doubts felt about the official design, they were concealed and the committee went ahead receiving and examining the tenders, which had to be in by 10 July. Under the terms of the clause Cole had had inserted, Paxton was told that he would be allowed to persuade a contractor (if he could) to submit an estimate for his plan, under the face-saving euphemism of its being an 'improvement' upon the official one, but that such an estimate had to be an addition to and not a substitute for it.

In this computerized, electronic, jet-flying age the time allowed for contractors to tender seems woefully short, and the time allowed to Paxton and his chosen team impossibly brief; but the history of the Crystal Palace demonstrates again and again that the age of the gas-lamp and the steam locomotive could often outstrip the age of the computer.

Although no records exist to prove or disprove it, it is fair to assume Paxton had had preliminary discussions with his chosen contractors, whom he knew well, before the official invitation to tender was issued, but in effect they had the inside of a week in which to calculate the quantities and labour for two buildings, each bigger than the biggest cathedral in London and one on a new principle of construction. As far as Paxton's plan was concerned this meant translating from what was in effect a dimensioned feasibility study, because Paxton was in no position to calculate the weights and quantities of iron, glass and other materials.

A further difficulty was that the day on which Paxton knew formally that he could ask contractors to tender happened to be the Saturday before the first day on which the Evangelical and Sabbatarian movements had succeeded in stopping the Sunday postal services. For the first time since 1784, when John Palmer's mail coaches had made daily interchanges possible, letters between London and Birmingham would take two days—as they all too often do today irrespective of the Sunday intervention. However, the Post Office had not then taken command of the infant electric telegraph system, which the public could use between the principal towns by courtesy of the railway companies and the excellent district messenger services. So the Wheatstone needles were set to motion in their galvanic dance (the language of the period is very infectious), and some of Paxton's important business friends arrived in London by the first train on Monday morning. The principal figures were Mr Chance of Chance Brothers, Birmingham, one of England's biggest glassmakers, and Mr Fox and Mr Henderson, contractors, engineers and ironmasters from nearby Smethwick.

Fox and Henderson had an office in Spring Gardens where they, their assistants and Paxton, Robert Chance and, occasionally, Henry Cole settled down to the job of getting out two complicated estimates in five days. Cole was invaluable in this as he went outside his brief as a member of the Executive Committee to give inside information of what the Building Committee wanted: this enabled them to concentrate on essentials. They had first to produce figures for the official design which would not look too superficial and spurious, and then give detailed costs for a plan which contained many unknown factors. With nothing more than a ready reckoner to help, they contrived to give chapter and verse for supplying and erecting 3,300 supporting columns, and nearly as many cylindrical pipes of similar dimensions to serve as combined foundations and drainage conduits; to these were added 2,224 principal girders (in all about 3,800 tons of cast and 700 tons of wrought iron), 600,000 cu. ft. of timber for joists, for flooring and to be cut into 24 miles of patent 'Paxton guttering' and 205 miles of glazing bar. Then there was the little item of 900,000 sq. ft. of sheet glass, between a third and a half of the country's total output in 1849, most of it in larger-sized panes than had been made before except in penny numbers for large mirrors or other special purposes. Nails, putty, paint, water pipes, drains, gas-fittings and other items had to be allowed for, though not in detail at this stage, together with such things as canvas covers to shut out unwanted sun and many yards of shuttering with movable louvres of unique form to let in needed air.

As originally planned the enclosed area amounted to 33,000,000 cu. ft., and Fox and Henderson offered to put the building up for £150,000, or for £79,800 if they could have the materials back after dismantling. In other words, considered as a permanent building it would cost one penny a cubic foot, but in the temporary form it would be only between a halfpenny and three-farthings a cubic foot. Translation of good Victorian ha'pence into their debased, devalued and decimalized equivalents of 1974 is not easy, but it can safely be said that no contractor today would dare tender at so low a price, nor could he undertake to put up such a building, enclosing nearly nineteen acres, in twenty-two weeks. This is what was achieved, and the processes of fitting-out and decorating was able to be started in the first week of January 1851.

Although the formal decision was not given until 26 July, the Building Committee did not take very long to decide once they had studied all the tenders, but one major alteration had to be made to the Paxton plan at this stage. Paxton had agreed to cover, or partly cover, the few small elms remaining on the site, but three very large old ones which stood nearly in the middle of it were not considered as they had been marked for felling. Colonel Sibthorp was still firing his ordnance, and to spike at least one of his guns Fox and Henderson were now asked if they would add the proposed transept with a vaulted roof high enough to enclose the big trees without extra cost. They agreed, and on 15 July the committee advised the Commissioners to accept Fox and Henderson's tender. This was informally done at once, but one hurdle remained: Charles Fox was asked to see Lord Granville who told him that as the Commission had not yet received parliamentary approval of its charter of incorporation no legally binding contract could be signed until later. Would Fox and Henderson accept Lord Granville's word of honour and go ahead without a contract and without any prospect of payment for some weeks? Fox unhesitatingly accepted Lord Granville's word, the Commission formally accepted the tender on the 26th and Fox and Henderson took possession of the site, with an initial gang of thirty-nine workmen, on 30 July.

Initial work on the site could not amount to more than levelling and marking out until the detailed working drawings had been prepared and the foundry and glassworks began pouring out the material. The workmen's first task, indeed, was to enclose the whole area of 26 acres with a stout timber palisade, 8 ft. high. The Crystal Palace may be regarded as the world's first pre-fabricated building made from mass-produced parts, and there is a nice link between it and the first mass-produced motor car, the Model T Ford. The vertical posts and horizontal planks of the palisade were carefully chosen for dimensions so that they could later be used to make the joists and floorboards of the finished building. Similarly, those Model T Fords which were not driven from the factory but dispatched by rail and ship were not fitted with floor-boards, but the stout wooden crates in which they were packed were assembled in such a way that they could be unbolted by the recipient to provide the necessary flooring material.

The addition of the three-stages-high transept with its semi-circular roof was not the only difference between the finished building and Paxton's original design published in the *Illustrated London News*. The rather clumsy verandas were removed and an extension added to the lower floor, on the north face, which gave an extra 48 ft. of width for a length of 936 ft. Discounting this extension, the width of the main building was 408 ft. and the length 1,848 ft., against the 515 ft. of St Paul's Cathedral. Height to the roof of the nave was 63 ft., and to the barrel roof over the new transept, 108 ft. Many of the contemporary drawings make it appear that the transept was in the middle of the building, but the configuration of the site and the position of the trees required it to be 48 ft. off-centre towards the west.

Charles Barry not unexpectedly claimed the much-admired semi-circular transept roof as his idea, but in his notes Paxton makes it clear that he thought of it in response to a strong hint from Cole that retaining the big trees would help sway the committee in favour. Whatever its origins the transept adds greatly to the appearance of the building by giving it a focal point of interest and freedom from monotony without making it too fussy in outline; and the building's appearance was further enhanced by the timely removal of the verandas.

In the early stages when Fox and Henderson were working the original plan towards its final form a flat-roofed transept to match the flat-roofed nave had been suggested, to which Paxton objected because, as he wrote:

> Mr Henderson suggested the transept; to this I at first objected; I did so on these grounds—namely, that as the Exhibition was to be a fair competition of skill for all nations, I held it to be right and fair that each exhibitor should have an equal advantage as regards position—which they would not have with the introduction of a transept; another objection I entertained was that it could not stand in the centre of the building as the ground plan was then arranged; but the moment Mr Henderson said it would impart strength and an air of solidity to the building I assented to its intro-

44

duction. . . . In order to get the tender in it was necessary the building should cover the exact space marked out by the Building Committee; but in conforming to this plan the transept was obliged to be put into one side of the building, for the purpose of avoiding the great trees which now stand within it, but which according to the tender sent in was to be an open court. At one of the meetings of the Building Committee it was suggested that the transept should include the great trees ... we promised to see what could be done. I went direct with Mr Fox to his office and while he rearranged the ground plan so as to bring the trees into the centre of the building, I was contriving how they should be covered. At length I hit upon the plan of covering the transept with a circular roof ... and made a sketch of it, which was copied that night by one of the draughtsmen, in order that I might have it to show Mr Brunel, whom I had agreed to meet on the ground the next day. Before nine o'clock the next morning Mr Brunel called at Devonshire House and brought me the heights of all the great trees; in the note containing the measurements Mr Brunel wrote thus: 'I mean to win with our plan, but I have thought it right to give your beautiful plan all the advantages it is susceptible of.' ... I have been led into these minute details first to show that the circular roof was designed by myself and not by Mr Barry, as currently reported; secondly to show the kindness and liberality of Mr Brunel.

In the event it was found better not to shift the ground plan of the building so as to bring the trees into the centre, but to be content with having the transept slightly off-centre. Very few people noticed.

Preparation of the working drawings was a monumental task performed almost single-handed by Charles Fox working, as he recorded, for about eighteen hours a day for seven weeks. As each detail was drawn it was passed to Henderson who supervised, where appropriate, the pattern-making, the subsequent foundry work and hydraulic strength-testing of the prototype major components. William Cubitt was invited to attend the tests in order to satisfy himself on behalf of the Commissioners that the margins of safety were adequate.

When it is realized that these working drawings, which are beautifully executed, include even such minor details as the dimensions and shape of the wheels to rotate the shafts, bevels and worm gears to open or close the S-shaped ventilating louvres, or the method for assembling the delicate gallery rails, one can but conclude that Fox was as much of a glutton for work as Paxton. Charles Fox had come up in much the same way as Robert Stephenson. He was born in 1810 and at fifteen years of age was bound pupil to the Swedish-born John Ericsson who laid claim with Charles Pettit Smith as inventor of the screw propeller. Fox helped with the construction of Ericsson's ingenious but unsuccessful locomotive, *Novelty*, which contended against Stephenson's *Rocket* at the Rainhill Trials in 1829; from this he went on to become one of the assistant engineers to the London & Birmingham Railway which he left to start his own business in 1839.

Fortunately the great interest created by the Crystal Palace led Fox and Henderson to publish a limited edition of the working drawings in 1852. Only a few copies of this rare book survive, but the Victoria and Albert Museum authorities have had a fine reprint produced for sale by the Stationery Office, and a professional draughtsman who was asked to examine the drawings said that he would not undertake to do similar work in less than eight months.

It is often pointed out that large railway stations or train sheds were already being roofed with large-span iron and glass structures and that consequently Paxton, Fox, Henderson and the rest were doing nothing new in the Crystal Palace. But these structures were supported by brick and masonry walls, with individual sections given portal bracing by arched girders or spandrel brackets between vertical and horizontal members. The Crystal Palace was the first purely rectilinear metal-framed building, without external walls or internal portal bracing, dependent for its lateral stability entirely on rigidly connected vertical columns and light horizontal girders, with a minimum of diagonal bracing in parts of greatest stress by wrought-iron ties. It was, therefore, an entirely new concept and not surprisingly there were experts ready to say it would not do. One of these experts was the Astronomer Royal, Sir George Airey, who did his sums and pronounced with oracular finality that the Crystal Palace could not possibly stand against a wind of 'moderate force'. As it was this same Sir George Airey who later pronounced with equal certainty that Bouch's Tay Bridge *would* stand as no wind would exert more than 10 pounds per square inch pressure upon it, it is as well that the builders of the Crystal Palace paid no heed to him and continued to have faith in the design.

Had the Crystal Palace been built in 1950 rather than 1850 both the vertical and the horizontal members of the framework would almost certainly have been those ugly but essential articles of modern construction, rolled steel joists. The structure therefore would have been slightly stronger for an equivalent amount of metal, or equally strong for a lesser weight, but aesthetically it would have been less pleasing. Also, the vertical members could not have served as rainwater pipes in the way Paxton's hollow cast columns did. Much of the beauty of the Crystal Palace came from its visible skeleton, which was delicate-looking and decorative without being fussy.

The Bessemer and Siemens processes which make possible the large-scale production of mild steel did not reach commercial practicability until the late 1860s, and the material available for the Crystal Palace was iron, cast or wrought. Both forms of the metal had, of course, been known for centuries, but it is too easily overlooked that the coke-smelting process of making cast iron cheaply and reliably on a large scale only dates back to the 1770s. It was Abram Darby's invention of this process at Coalbrookdale in 1709 which laid the foundation for the nineteenth-century iron age, and that other stand-by of the Industrial Revolution, rolled sheet iron, of which Brunel proposed to make his monstrous dome, was of even more recent origin. In 1850 there were still plenty of people who had been brought up in an era when no such thing as a sheet-iron bucket, or similarly commonplace object, existed. Eighteenth-century wooden or leather buckets now seem quaint objects to fill with flowers and rhapsodize over, but were matters of stern necessity when they were made.

The use of cast iron as a building material dates from the late eighteenth century, and was first seen on a big scale in a large spinning mill built for Messrs Phillips and Lee in Salford in 1801. It was a Boulton & Watt construction with cast iron used for the columns and beams, as well as for window frames, staircases and other details, with the object of reducing the risk of fire. For the same reason it was one of the earliest large buildings to be lit by coal-gas. Naked bat's-wing burners might not satisfy a modern factory inspector, but at least they could not be knocked over as candles and lamps so often were.

By 1850 engineers and builders were well aware of the limitations of cast iron. It is strong in compression but weak in tension, and attempts were made to overcome the weakness by fixing wrought-iron tie-rods to relieve the tension stresses in the lower flanges of cast-iron beams or girders. The principle was as sound as the similar pre-stressing of concrete beams, but the methods of attaching the tie-bars were sometimes unreliable as was fatally shown in 1847 when such a composite girder collapsed under the weight of a loaded train crossing Stephenson's bridge over the River Dee on the Chester and Holyhead Railway. The use of cast iron for the horizontal members of the Crystal Palace was criticized by some engineers, but they were not required to take any greater bending loads than those imposed by part of the weight of the gallery floors and the exhibits and people on them. For these loads the slender-looking lattice girders were perfectly adequate: they were made in two sections with the heavier ones tested to stand fifteen tons bending strain at mid-point, whilst those for the lighter work were tested to nine tons.

Production of pig-iron for casting rose from 258,000 tons in 1800 to 2¾ million tons in 1850 so the Crystal Palace's demand for about 5,000 tons did not pose any particular difficulty, but the demand for 900,000 sq. ft. of window glass was much less easily met particularly as the design called for most of it to be in panes 4 ft. 1 in. long. Paxton flatly refused to use overlapping panes which were such an incurable source of leaks in conventional glasshouses.

Until 1845 when Sir Robert Peel relieved it of excise duty glass had been taxed. This had driven the best manufacturers of ornamental and drinking glasses to move their business to Waterford in Ireland (where glass was duty-free), and kept the makers of window and mirror glass technically lagging behind their Continental counterparts. Cast and rolled plate glass, now universally used for windows and mirrors, was then only made in penny numbers and was very expensive. Most windows were glazed with crown glass which could not be made in the size Paxton specified. The method had remained unaltered for centuries: having taken a suitable lump of glass from the furnace on the end of his blow-pipe the craftsman blew and twirled it quickly into a large bubble; the blow-pipe was then rapidly rotated to-and-fro along the extended arms of a special chair in which the workman sat so that centrifugal force spun the molten globe into a more or less flat disc. When solidified and broken from the pipe the disc could be cut into window panes (seldom completely flat which is why old windows appear to have more 'life' than dead-flat plate glass), with the central 'bullion' or 'bull's eye' reserved for cheap cottage windows or pavement lights. The physical limitations of the method made it impossible to spin discs of much more than four feet in diameter, from which it is not possible to cut usable panes of more than about 28-30 in. long.

Paxton's plans called for the majority of the panes to be 49 in. long and 10 in. wide and the need was met by the use of sheet glass which, like plate glass, had occasionally been made since the seventeenth century but only on a very limited scale. It was only in 1832 that Chance Brothers had started quantity production of sheet glass. Like crown glass much depended on the skill of the worker who blew, rolled and manipulated his lumps of molten glass upon a heated metal table so as to produce a cylinder which, if he were skilful, could be as much as 2 ft. in diameter. Whilst still plastic this had to be taken from the pipe, opened at each end and rapidly cut along its length whereupon, if the degree of plasticity was right, it fell open upon the iron surface and cooled into a flat sheet needing only to be annealed, cut true and polished along its edges. The large size and great number of sheets required stretched Chance's resources to their limits and the *Official Popular Guide* to the Exhibition reported that '... the short time within which the immense quantity necessary had to be supplied, demanded the employment of numerous additional hands, and workmen had to be sought from abroad to assist in the completion of the order within the requisite time.'

We are so accustomed today to the sight of that most unlovely building material, concrete, that it is difficult to realize that it also was something of a novelty in 1850. In the form of the mis-called 'Roman cement' mixed with Thames gravel it was used for the foundations of the Crystal Palace where it was kept decently out of sight and where, indeed, it remains to this day beneath the turf of Hyde Park. Once the delicate job of levelling and setting-out had been done the foundations could scarcely have been simpler or quicker to make.

The foundations consisted in effect of a series of cast-iron base-plates and sockets, rather like inverted flat-headed mushrooms, embedded on concrete in suitable pits or excavations 24 ft. apart in parallel rows running the length of the building from west to east, with the rows 24, 48 or 72 ft. apart according to the parts of the structure to rise above them. The skyward-pointing hollow 'stems' of the inverted mushrooms were shaped and flanged to receive the end sockets of the similarly shaped and flanged columns, which were dropped into them until the flanges met and could be bolted together with four $1\frac{1}{4}$ in. Whitworth bolts and nuts. At, or just below, ground level, according to the lie of the land, horizontally projecting hollow arms were cast integrally with the base-plate stems, and these received cast-iron pipes of 8 in. outside diameter to carry away the rain-water which was in turn carried to them from the roofs down the hollow columns. The horizontal drainage pipes running from column-base to column-base along the length of the building discharged into a large-bore communal trans-verse main drainage pipe at the east end of the building towards which the whole structure imperceptibly tilted. The depths of the concrete emplacements to which the base-plates were bolted varied from 2 ft. to nearly 5 ft. according to the nature of the ground, and the method of setting out the foundations is best described in the contractors' words:

> The centre line of each row of columns was set out by means of a theodolite, and the distance from centre to centre of the columns was measured by means of rods of well-seasoned pine, on which were fixed two pieces of gun-metal, the distance between which was exactly 24 ft. A stake was driven into the ground to mark the position of each column and a pin was driven into the top of the stake to mark the centre of the column. In proceeding to sink the pit to receive the concrete on which the column was to stand, it was necessary to remove the stake. In order, however, to preserve the centre point, two stakes were driven into the ground at a distance of 6 ft. from the column. One of these stakes was in line with the row of columns, and the other in a line at right angles to it. A right-angled triangle, formed of three pieces of wood, was laid upon the three stakes, and a saw-kerf in the right angle was fitted to the pin in the stake which marked the centre point for the column. Two other pins were driven into the two new stakes at the points marked by two saw-kerves in the sides of the triangle. Another

51

triangle was prepared, similar to the first, with the exception of one angle which was cut to fit the sectional form of the column. The centre stake was then pulled out, and a pit sunk to the requisite depth to obtain a good foundation, and filled with concrete to the proper level. The lower portion of the column, with its base-plate was then bedded on the concrete, and its position accurately adjusted by means of the second triangle above-mentioned. Owing to the ground having a slight fall from west to east, the whole building was constructed on an inclination of 1 in. in 24 ft. and the columns deviate from the perpendicular in the same proportion ...

It is usual to refer to the roofs as flat (except, of course, for the arched transept), and so they appeared to be from the outside. The areas were much too large for flat roofing, however, and the parapets concealed a series of shallow ridge-roofs spaced 8 ft. between the valleys. The ridge rafters were of unusually slender dimensions, and the greatest weight of glass was taken on the patent Paxton gutters on which the lower edge of each pane rested. The Paxton gutters were carried across the bays and at each 24 ft. interval where the cross girders ran at right angles to the ridges and valleys the Paxton gutters rested upon and discharged into flat-bottomed wooden channels attached to the upper members

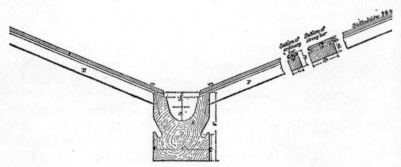

A section of the Paxton gutter and glass roof

The 'Beloved Angel'. A pencil drawing by Queen Victoria of Prince Albert, dated 1840

The Man Behind the Scenes: Sir Henry Cole, circa 1875, from the mosaic portrait flanking the main staircase of the Victoria and Albert Museum

Joseph Paxton in 1835, by Henry Perronet Briggs

Leading the Opposition: Colonel Sibthorp, by Alfred Crowquill

The Royal Commissioners at Work. Sir Robert Peel stands behind Prince Albert's chair; Joseph Paxton emphasizes a point with his index finger on the table; Henry Cole is the third standing figure from the left

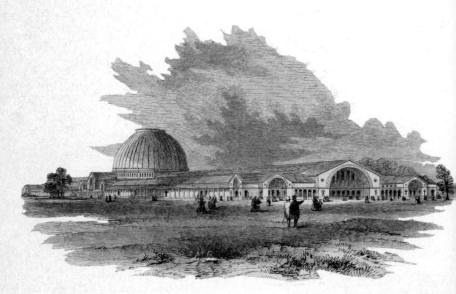

Palace of Brick. One of the three published drawings of Building Committee's design

Rejected Designs. Interior and exterior views of two of the 245 designs which the Building Committee rejected

A View of the Works. One of a series of engravings which appeared in the *Illustrated London News*

Upper Portion of a Column. This illustration omits the keys which, without rivets, tightened the girders into the snugs

aising the First Pair of Transept Ribs. As the width of the ribs was greater than
he space they were to span, they had to be hoisted in this inclined position

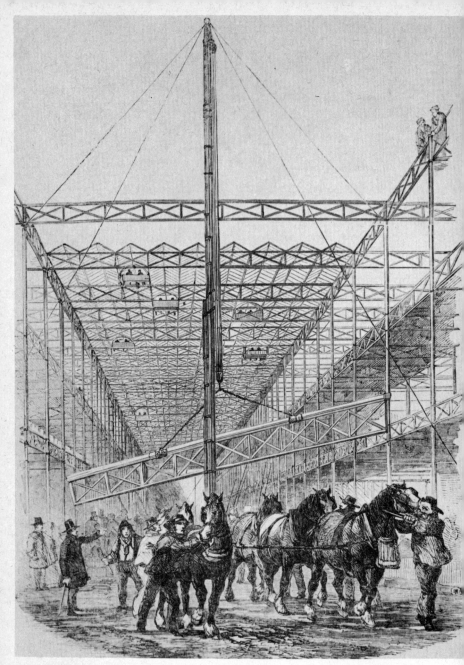

Raising the Trusses. In the words of the contractors, 'A pair of "shears", formed of two scaffold poles supported by guy ropes, was erected and a pair of blocks suspended from it. The rope from the blocks passed through a snatch block and was carried along in a horizontal direction. One or more horses were harnessed to this rope, and by walking forward in a straight line, raised the girder.' Notice the glaziers in the roof

Glazing Wagon. This 'impression' probably owes more to the artist's imagination than to his knowledge of practical mechanics

The Sash-Bar Machine. The workman is feeding in planks which emerge at the left of the machine as several grooved and bevelled bars

Making Glass. A view of the Chance Bros. works where an additional thirty French blowers were taken on to produce the glass sheets

of the girders; these troughs in turn carried the water into the supporting columns down which it ran to the foundation pipes and finally to the storm sewer in Kensington Road.

The figure opposite shows that the gutters had a semi-circular central channel, with sloping edges for the glass to rest upon, and two smaller channels one on either side. Rain-water trickled into the central trough, whilst condensate trickled down the insides of the panes to be drawn by capillary attraction into the side channels which conducted it out of harm's way.

All the machining of the woodwork was done on the site and the Paxton gutters, so simple and ingenious, worked to a nicety; but until the public had proof, fear of damage to exhibits by condensation was a bogey which the dwindling band of opponents exploited to the utmost. While Charles Fox laboured over the working drawings, and for some time afterwards, Paxton patiently answered criticism in the Press, and on the condensation question he finally quoted a letter from a Derbyshire landowner for whom he had designed a conservatory with his patent roofing. This satisfied customer reported that he kept his books, best pictures and finally his piano in the conservatory as he found it was drier than any room in the house. In writing of the building design in general Paxton took the opportunity to pay the following tribute:

> I have stated to you that the *Victoria regia* was the immediate cause of my sending in a design for the Crystal Palace; but the Crystal Palace does not derive its *origin* from that noble plant. No, it owes its erection to a nobler work of nature, the noble Duke whom I have had the honour and pleasure to serve for more than a quarter of a century. It is to his fostering hand I owe all I possess.

5 The Glass

The *Official Popular Guide*'s statement that 'numerous additional hands were demanded and that workmen had to be sought from abroad' to help make the glass in the short time available, glosses over the fact that the ludicrous excise duty which Sir Robert Peel abolished had allowed Continental glass-makers so much headway that the English firms became heavily dependent on foreign craftsmen to expand production after the duty was lifted. This was certainly true of Chance Brothers and Company of Spon Lane, Birmingham, whose foreman-manager of their 'patent plate' works was a Belgian named Biver, whilst most of their blowers in the sheet-glass department were French. Ultimately an additional thirty French blowers were employed to cope with the Crystal Palace order, and they were paid at the then-generous rate of £18* a month with their lodging and heating costs paid by the firm.

The restrictive effects of the excise duty on the glass industry were well illustrated by Charles Dickens who wrote in *Household Words* in February 1851 :

The great demand occasioned by the immediate fall in

---

* The generosity may be measured by comparing this with the wages of the workmen on the site which, on average, were 28s. a week.

price [after the repeal of the Duty] produced this effect on the Thames Plate Glass works. They now manufacture as much plate glass per week as was turned out in the days of the Excise in the same time by all the works in the country put together. The Excise incubi clogged the operations of the workmen, and prevented every sort of improvement in the manufacture. They put their 'gauges' into the 'metal' (or mixed materials) before it was put into the pot. They overhauled the paste when it was taken out of the fire, and they applied their foot-rules to the sheets after the glass was annealed. The duty was collected during the various stages of manufacture half a dozen times and amounted to 300 per cent. No improvement was according to law, and the Excise man put his veto upon every attempt of the sort. In the old time the mysterious mixer could not have exercised his secret vocation for the benefit of his employers, and the demand for glass was so small that Mr Blake's admirable polishing machine would never have been invented. Nor could plate glass ever have been used for transparent flooring, or for door panels, or for a thousand other purposes to which it is now advantageously and economically applied.

To a generation accustomed to huge buildings with walls of plate glass made in sheets of almost any size the architect chooses to command, the difficulties of using glass in a similar fashion 150-odd years ago are almost incomprehensible.

Cast or cast-and-rolled plate glass was certainly being made in significant amounts as Dickens's account shows, and Chance Brothers had a 'patent plate' works at Camden Town, in addition to their Birmingham factory, in the 1840s. Here, under Robert Chance's supervision and in the face of many setbacks, attempts were made to produce rolled plate in commercial quantities by a process patented jointly with Henry Bessemer of steel-making fame. Expensive failure followed expensive failure and the association between

Chance and Bessemer was severed in April 1851.

Had it succeeded the Bessemer-Chance process would have produced large sheets of plate glass clear enough for window or mirror glazing with less need for the expensive polishing process required with the ordinary cast plate of the period. Apart from troubles with the new form of reverberatory furnace, even when the rolling machinery was working properly it was found impossible to produce glass thinner than $\frac{3}{16}$ in.: this would have been intolerably heavy for glazing large roof areas. Also, unlike crown glass and most sheet glass (which was not dead flat until the edges were trimmed), the rolled plates could not be stacked one on top of another for annealing, but had to be passed one at a time through the annealing kiln or stacked with spacers between the sheets which often gave rise to distortion. Nevertheless, the financial attraction of dispensing with skilled and (relatively) highly-paid blowers was enough to encourage Messrs Chance to persevere with their patent plate department after the breach with Bessemer.

Cast plate glass was easier to make but more expensive to finish, and James Hartley, who was granted a patent in 1847, also tendered for the Crystal Palace glazing. His rough plate glass required polishing before it could be used for windows but was suitable for skylights or glass roofs in the unpolished state. It could be made down to $\frac{1}{8}$ in. in thickness and Hartley's tender offered it in plates of 62 in. by 21 in. which would have reduced the amount of framing in the roof whilst doubling the weight of glass by comparison with Chance's 16 oz. sheet glass. Both Paxton's original design and Fox and Henderson's final version were based on the weight of the 16 oz. glass, and there was also some doubt about annealing Hartley's cast plate. Consequently his tender was rejected.

As Robert Lucas Chance had been called in to help with the initial planning, and as Paxton knew from his Chatsworth glasshouses exactly what the Birmingham firm could and could not do, it seems likely that Hartley never stood much chance. Indeed, a look at the detailed dimensions of

the Crystal Palace reveals that the fundamental dimension
of 8 ft., with the resultant 24 ft. spacing of columns and
bays, and so on up to the 72 ft. span of the nave, was determined by the size of glass Chance Brothers could guarantee
to supply quickly and cheaply.

In designing the ridge and valley roofing for the Great
Conservatory and the Lily House at Chatsworth, where the
object was to retain rather than to dispel condensation,
Paxton had found that if the slope of the glass was one in
2½ or steeper the condensation would not form globules
large enough to drop from the pane but would slide down
to the bottom of the glass. This was the principle used in the
Crystal Palace to conduct the condensate into the side
channels of the Paxton gutters. Chance Brothers were able
to supply panes of more than 4 ft. 6 in. in length only at
disproportionately greater cost than those below that size,
because of the much higher proportion of failures. The
greatest length they were able to produce of guaranteed
quality, and uniform weight of 16 oz. per sq. ft., at reasonable cost was 49 in. Allowing for the width of the ridge
beams, panes 49 in. long inclined at one foot in two foot
six made the distance between valleys 8 ft. which thus
became the basic module for the whole structure. With the
edges untrimmed the 49 in. panes were just over 30 in. wide,
and consequently three 10 in. widths were produced from
each.

A modern Paxton would be able to fix his dimensions
first knowing that glassmakers could supply sheets of any
size he wanted within reason, and it is an interesting comment on the state of the art in 1850 that things had to be
calculated from the size of the panes, but the evidence of
J. F. Chance's *History of Chance Brothers and Company*
and other sources make it clear that this was so. An interesting oddity of the dimensions of the Crystal Palace is that
the total length of 1,848 ft. was an inside measurement but
the greatest external length, over the widest parts of the
columns, was 1,851 ft. Whether this happy match with the

year of the Exhibition was fortuitous or planned it is not possible to say.

It would be unfair to other contenders for the Exhibition building to claim that Paxton's was the only plan for a glass and iron structure. Amongst the 245 rejected designs was one for an iron-framed glass house submitted by Turner of Dublin. He was no amateur for he had already built a great palm house (or 'stove' as hot-houses were then often called) at Kew Gardens, but his domed offering for the Exhibition was judged impracticable and its estimated cost of £300,000 prohibitive.

It was Chance Brothers' ability to supply the glass quickly and cheaply which helped clinch the acceptance of Paxton's plan. Although their fame was later to rest chiefly on their optical glass (their first multi-lensed lighthouse lantern was shown at the Great Exhibition) their success with this huge glazing contract was of no small benefit to their reputation. The only drawback, apart from some undefined trouble with the French workmen, was that too much glass was broken by careless handling on the site. The exact amount of breakage is not known, but it is said that on one occasion a workman used a stack of the special crates of glass as a working platform and caused the whole pile to collapse. If the breakages are put conservatively at a tenth, Chance Brothers supplied over a million square feet in little more than ten weeks, and when the glazing work was at its height in January 1851 they produced 63,000 panes in a fortnight.

6 The Method

It is unfortunate that the photographic processes in use in 1850 and 1851 were not fast enough to capture scenes in which there was any movement. Except for portrait work the original daguerreotypes, taken on small silvered plates from which it was not possible to take positive prints, were being ousted by the calotype process. This had been devised by William Fox Talbot and was not only slightly faster but provided paper negatives from which paper positive prints could be taken; but exposures of ten seconds or more were needed, and the only surviving photographs of the Crystal Palace are calotypes taken before or after the public had come or gone. They are mostly interior views, but the blurred outlines of the flags in the few surviving exterior photographs show how slow the process was and why moving human figures could not be included. A photograph of the 'opening ceremony' is often reproduced, but it does not depict the scene on 1 May 1851 but a much later occasion after the Palace had been removed and rebuilt. The half-tone process of mass-reproduction of photographs was also unknown at that time.

Therefore there are no photographs of the construction work in progress, and apart from some private sketches which may await discovery in attic or cellar somewhere, we have to rely on the many drawings published in the

Illustrated London News, Punch, the *Official Popular Guide* and elsewhere.

The business of making these prints was well organized but suffered from certain weaknesses which must be taken into account when looking at them. The first shortcoming was that the artist was not his own engraver, and no matter how skilled the latter might be some of the nuances of the original work were lost and mistakes could creep in. Indeed, it is remarkable how accurately the artist's work was reproduced, particularly when working against time for the production of a weekly journal, because it became the practice to speed the engraving process of the larger drawings by cutting the originals into four or more pieces so that four or more engravers could work simultaneously cutting four or more blocks, which were then locked together into one forme for printing, each representing only a part of the picture which the individual engravers probably never saw *in toto* until the proofs were pulled.

Quite apart from this piecemeal method of engraving, another shortcoming was that most artists were ignorant of mechanical details, quite often guessed at what they could not see clearly and often guessed wrongly. The most elementary mistakes could be made, a typical example of which is to be found in the picture of an early railway scene which includes a locomotive with *coupled* driving wheels of *unequal* diameter. Though no mistakes as glaring as this are to be found in them, some of the details in the engravings of the construction work on the Crystal Palace are inaccurate.

The most serious shortcoming is that there are no published illustrations of the early stages of construction, apart from imaginary ones, because the Royal Commission tried to commit the folly of excluding the Press. After the roasting they had had the Commissioners were very ready to share the habitual governmental dislike of newspapers, and they found it hard to forgive some of the Sibthorp-type insults which had been hurled at them. Henry Cole saw how wrong-headed they were and wrote:

It was seriously proposed to exclude the Press! I urged that this would be an unprecedented step! that the interest of the Exhibition was to attract the Press to come and report on everything that was going on as much as possible. Instead of making the Press pay for entrance, the very reverse would be the safer policy in my opinion, and I entreated the Commissioners not to make so fatal and suicidal a rule. A member of the Commission exclaimed, 'Alas! we are a Press-ridden people', and then the Commissioners present gave up the proposal, and Dilke said to me 'You get your way when you are in a minority of one.' But I had after-wards to contend for the freest admission of the Press —and at last on the 11th of February, Lord Granville agreed to admit the artist of the *Illustrated London News* to draw.

It is not easy therefore to account for some of the draw-ings, which were published before 11 February 1851, except on the supposition that they were done surreptitiously by *Illustrated London News* artists who mingled with the crowds after the works were opened to sightseers towards the end of September 1850. This may account for certain discre-pancies, such as the picture of the raising of the first tran-sept ribs, on 4 December, showing winches and sheerlegs in use whilst the written description refers to cranes. Even the high price of five shillings did not deter the sightseers, and on average about two hundred a day came to watch the work. The contractors complained that they got in the way but realized their goodwill was important, and the admission money was paid into an accident and sick-pay fund for the workmen.

In the early stages of levelling, assembling timber and preparing the foundations there was no particular attraction about the work, but on 26 September the first upright column was put into place and from that moment the building grew at an astonishing pace and attracted more and more on-lookers. As it grew, more hands were employed to accelerate it further. At the beginning of September only the original 39 men were at work on the site; a month later there were 419; by 1 November 1,476 were employed; the highest figure of 2,260 was reached by 6 December 1850; by 3 January when the last panes of glass were going in the number had dwindled to 2,112, and thereafter those employed on painting and fitting out averaged about 1,700 until the work was finished.

All the work of erection was done by man- or horse-power, and although there are references to a single-derrick crane it seems that the components of the entire framework were raised by sheerlegs and put together without scaffolding. There was one steam engine of six indicated horse-power on the site, but it was not used for hoisting and was kept busy driving machines for sawing, planing, routing and shaping all the woodwork, and for boring, cutting and punching the light metal-work used for tie-bars, gallery rails and other items.

The steam engine, not shown in any of the engravings, was almost certainly a 'portable'; that is, it consisted of a locomotive-type horizontal fire-tube boiler and fire-box, surmounted by a single-cylinder engine with twin flywheels, which also served as belt-pulleys, all carried on wheels and with a swivelling fore-carriage and shafts so that it could be moved by horse haulage. These 'portables', coming into widespread use for driving threshing machines and other tackle, were easily developed into self-moving engines and thus were the ancestors of the familiar traction-engines of a slightly later period.

Though none of the contemporary pictures show this solitary mechanical aid, a number show one or more of the machines it drove. It may be necessary to allow for a little inaccuracy in them but they illuminate most vividly a state of affairs which would throw any twentieth-century factory- or safety-inspector into a fit. Long, unguarded leather belts into which any preoccupied workman or spectator might walk drove equally unguarded circular saws, planing machines and other contrivances whilst planks and other obstacles lay around ready to trip the unwary into their whirling teeth or gnashing jaws. Various views of the assembling and glazing processes show unsecured planks resting across girders, with unsecured ladders resting against them; and men and boys working on those planks and climbing those ladders with heavy loads have, of course, no safety harnesses or 'hard hats'.

The *Official Popular Guide* proudly quoted how many tons of this or yards of that went into the building but preserved a discreet silence about accidents. That there must have been accidents is certain, as the setting-up of the accident fund tacitly admits, but mercifully there do not appear to have been any deaths. One of the least pleasing features of the early Victorian railway and other construction was that pressure of time and money on the contractors, and the lure of piece-work among the 'navvies', led to total disregard for safety and a terrible record of mutilation and death. The tendency had already been apparent before the death of Thomas Telford, whose roads, bridges, harbours and canals had been constructed without the loss of a single life. In his respected old age the great engineer protested against 'such haste, pregnant as it was and ever will be with risks'; but few paid heed and according to L. T. C. Rolt's *Victorian Engineering*, the five-years-long task of blasting and digging the three-mile Woodhead tunnel through treacherous Pennine strata maimed or killed more men in proportion to the numbers engaged than 'any of the major battles of the century, Waterloo not excepted'. That the building of the Crystal Palace, one of the hastiest of the hasty works Telford deplored, killed nobody is attributable to the fact that at least one of the contracting partners, usually Henderson, but frequently Fox and Chance as well, was on the site to supervise each day's work.

It is this element of personal supervision by the 'bosses' which explains so much about the building of the Crystal Palace which would otherwise be inexplicable. In 1975 a firm of contractors small enough to have working drawings, quantity-surveying, pattern-making and foundry work done, or directly supervised, by the joint owners of the concern would almost certainly be considered too small to handle so important a contract. By the standards of 1850, however, Fox and Henderson's business was big business, but no business was then so complicated and impersonal that the principals did not attend to tasks which their modern counterparts feel obliged to leave to underlings. With all possible respect to Fox and Henderson's direct business descendants, Freeman, Fox and Partners the famous consulting engineers and designers, the present day equivalent of Mr Fox would be unlikely to sit for eighteen hours a day at the drawing board, nor would a modern Mr Henderson assume the guise of a site foreman and supervise the vital stages of erection.

Modern big business is generally unable to work as Victorian business did, and even when it can it generally does not do so for a variety of reasons not all of which are valid. Many of these invalid reasons, alas, are connected with status, for in our own way we are just as snobbish as the Victorians. The modern Mr Fox, for example, could not answer a business letter in his own hand as it would not give the correct air of efficiency and importance to the recipient. An electric tape-recorder, a typewriter, also electric and preferably with proportional spacing, an electric copier and a highly-paid secretary to work them all must be used, so that allowing for amortization of capital and the typist's wages the cost of each business letter is not less than £1. Worse, although all the machines are supposed to, and in a sense do, aid efficiency the letter will actually take longer to 'write' than it did in the days of pen-and-ink and the copying-press, when businessmen, statesmen and rulers nearly always drafted, and often fair-copied, their own letters in long-hand. How right Queen Victoria was to refuse to read typewritten documents in the last decade of her life.

Similarly it would be *infra dig* for the latter-day Mr Fox to prepare working drawings with his own hands. Not only would it be *infra dig*, it would give clients the wrong impression *and* waste the expensive services of the drawing office which, for a firm of Fox and Henderson's size would probably cost some £25,000 a year today in amortization, wages and proportion of rent. Parkinson's law would apply and two senior and two junior draughtsmen would be employed on the job the original Mr Fox did single-handed, but as they certainly would not be expected to work eighteen hours a day for seven weeks on end they would not do the job so quickly.

Nor would it be thought right today to design and put up a big building like the Crystal Palace without a prolonged and complex series of calculations and tests, which would almost certainly involve the use of a computer. Therefore the contractors of 1975 would be better informed than their forebears about stresses, margins of safety, dimensions of parts and other factors which engineers of the Stephenson, Brunel, Fox and Henderson breed worked out by rule of thumb and the instinctive 'eye' of the craftsman, possibly, but not certainly, aided by a slide-rule. Both methods can err and the errors can maim and kill, but despite the elaboration of ingenious modern scientific equipment, and the skills of those who use it, the new ways take longer than the old. There is little doubt there still are instinctive engineers about who can tell at a glance, or from experience, that such-and-such will do but that so-and-so might not, but because of the financial stakes involved few will risk taking their word for it. The figures must be checked by an expert, preferably one with letters after his name, and then checked again before being accepted, not by an individual but by a board, a committee or a local authority so that responsibility cannot be pinned upon one man should anything go wrong—as it was upon poor Thomas Bouch when his Tay Bridge fell down.

With his armoury of scientific and mechanical aids the modern engineer can perform feats beyond the imagination, let alone the capabilities, of the early Victorians; but over many less advanced, but still, to them, untried areas they could act with speed and vigour which now seem astounding. The low price of labour was obviously an important factor, but it is a mistake to assume that the labour was dirt-cheap and powerless. It is now part of working-class myth-ology that trade unions were illegal in the last century, but although they were much more restricted and discriminated against than they are now, they existed and had grown since the supposedly wicked and reactionary Tory govern-ment of Lord Liverpool legalized them in 1824. With or without union help Victorian working men—and women— were sometimes quite as ready to go on strike as their modern counterparts; but there was in fact only one strike during the erection of the Crystal Palace. This arose from a dispute about piece-work rates paid to the glaziers which was quickly settled.

Although the rectilinear framing of the Crystal Palace was apparently simple, its design posed a number of problems which had to be solved mostly by techniques which were new, or nearly so. In the first place, apart from nails in the woodwork, putty in the glasswork and rivets attaching some of the flanges and ties in the ironwork, the whole thing was put together with nuts and bolts like a gargantuan child's Meccano toy. This may seem hardly worth remarking upon in 1975, but in 1850 the standardized bolt and nut, machine-made and interchangeable, was still relatively new and a great many engineers had served their apprenticeships under masters who taught them to make wedges and keys for components which could not conveniently be riveted.

It is usual to refer to the Crystal Palace as an iron and glass building, but as it contained 600,000 cu. ft. of timber this is obviously an over-simplification. The design was such, however, that more or less of wood or iron could have been used, and the contractors later admitted that the main gutters into which the patent Paxton gutters discharged would have been better made of sheet iron. As it was the great demand on the timber industry, and the haste, obliged them to use a certain amount of unseasoned deal for the wooden troughs, and this warped.

Fox and Henderson's report pointed out that similar structures of any required size could be put up using galvanized iron in place of glass in the roofs, and with matchboarding or, again, sheet iron in the walls. Galvanized iron, still a very new material, was used for the ingenious adjustable S-shaped ventilating louvres, and it is rather curious that galvanized iron really was galvanized then; that is, the zinc was deposited by electrolytic or 'galvanic' action, whereas now the iron is coated by an apparently more primitive hot dipping process.

These ventilating louvres ran horizontally for several thousand feet along the bottom of the building at, or slightly below, floor level (according to the pitch of the ground) and correspondingly round the tops of the tiers behind ornamental trusses. The louvres were opened and closed by worm and wheel gear, several hundred feet at a time, according to the direction of the wind, and the arrangement ensured that warm air escaping from the upper vents drew in cooler air over the feet of the visitors on the ground floor. Therefore the familiar complaint of 'museum foot' was largely obviated. At ground-floor level the floorboards had half-inch gaps between them, partly to aid this air circulation and partly to make cleaning easier by allowing the 'sweeping machines', large multi-row brushes on wheels, to push the dust through the gaps. However, in the words of the report the machines were not needed on the ground floor because: '...the dresses of the female portion of the visitors performed this office in a very satisfactory manner.'

The efficacy of the ventilating system was attested by the Exhibition's most illustrious visitor, Queen Victoria, who paid more than forty visits. The Queen was apparently impervious to cold, greatly disliked heat and revelled in fresh air (quite contrary to the popular image of her and her age as 'stuffy'), as all those who were obliged to share with her the icy blasts and under-heated rooms of Balmoral so amply testify. Only twice in her journal did the Queen complain of heat at the Exhibition, and as one of those occasions, 28 June, 1851, was an exceptionally hot day the building was not entirely to blame. The Queen wrote:

> ... we went after breakfast to the Exhibition. ... I
> thought I should faint from the heat in the gallery,
> where we went to look at the English jewelry and plate.
> ... At 2 we left for Osborne and the heat in the train
> was *fearful* and made me really feel quite ill, but I was
> restored by the sea-breeze crossing over.

In *The Young Visiters* [*sic*], written when she was nine
years old, Daisy Ashford credits the Earl of Clincham's bath-
room, which by childish confusion with Hampton Court she
set in the 'private compartments' of the Crystal Palace, with
'many clever dodges of a costly nature', and the praise could
have been justly awarded to the real Palace itself. Many of
the clever dodges were not visible to the casual eye. For
example, the columns were all of the same external
diameter, so that all the horizontal girders could be of the
same length, but to save metal were cast with varying wall
thicknesses according to the loads they were to carry in
different parts of the building. Also, the male and female
parts of the columns where they were dropped into one
another or into the foundation sockets, together with the
flanges and the abutments for the cross girder trusses were
faced-off in the lathe or milling machine. This was an
expensive refinement but ensured no time had to be lost
on the site whilst men filed away the foundry 'rag', or
enlarged bolt holes. As the contractors wrote:

> ... all the columns are turned or faced at their ends,
> and the surfaces to which they are connected are also
> faced. This proceeding, although it may at first appear
> an unnecessary refinement, proved of the utmost
> importance in facilitating the rapid erection of the
> building, and effected a real economy. In fact, it is
> scarcely saying too much to affirm that the building
> could not otherwise have been erected in the short
> space of time granted for that purpose.

The lattice girders were also not as simple as they appeared and much thought had been put into their design. The lighter cast-iron girders were used only across the 24 ft. longitudinal bays, whilst the heavier ones crossed the 48 ft. span of the side aisles and galleries. Wrought iron was used for the 72 ft. width of the nave, and at the intersection of nave and transept the supporting columns, of the thickest section, were duplicated at the four corners. Of the girder design the contractors wrote:

> The first and most obvious duty of the girders is to support the roof, but their second and equally important duty is to give lateral stiffness to the whole structure. A girder of any form, provided its strength were sufficient, would have served to carry the roof, and might merely have rested on the top of the columns; but this would have given no lateral stiffness to the building, which might then have been levelled with the ground by the first storm. The contractors, therefore, in place of devising separate ... means of supporting the columns and preserving their perpendicularity, adopted the plan of distributing the metal of the girders in a form which should possess a much greater depth than is usually employed in cast-iron girders; and then, by firmly connecting the top and bottom of each girder to the columns, they at once obtained the desired result. The columns and girders thus connected may be compared with an ordinary four-legged table in which the side rails, which support the upper surface, are firmly fixed to the legs. A want of comprehension of this effect of the girders was the cause of a great waste of criticism on the presumed weakness of the structure.
>
> To obtain the requisite depth of girder, without unnecessarily increasing its weight or diminishing its thickness, it became necessary to cast it open, and the proper form of the apertures through it had to be decided. Various ornamental forms were proposed, but it was necessary to study strength as the first considera-

tion. The <u>trellis form</u> ... was adopted and its great superiority over any other will be perceived. It consists of a top and bottom rail or flange, united by four perpendicular struts and the diagonals ensure the load is supported over the two inmost struts ... if we view the form as a whole, we find that it combines both the trussed girder and the arch.

One aspect of the building is not mentioned in any of the eulogistic accounts of it. In all the deliberations of the Commission, the minutes of the committees, the cogitations of the contractors, the panegyrics of the Press or even the fulminations of Colonel Sibthorp one word is never used, one subject never mentioned, but fortunately the ground-plan survives to reassure us. No matter how superhuman their efforts, Paxton, Cole, Fox and Henderson, even the Prince himself recognized that others were but human, and adequate lavatories were provided near each of the three refreshment rooms on the ground floor.

Admission to the lavatories was free except to those near the south exit where 'retiring rooms' were also provided, with attendants, wash-basins, hot water and so forth. A threepenny charge was made and these lavatories took £2,441 of which £1,769 was reckoned to be profit. So impressed was the Society of Arts by this triumph of nature over frugality that the experiment was tried of putting similar conveniences on some streets of London, the world's richest capital city which, at that time, did not have a single public lavatory. The experiment did not pay and the idea of providing lavatories as a public service did not materialize until nearly thirty years later when the City Engineer, Sir William Haywood, came to the relief of the embattled citizens. We now take for granted one of the least known but most valuable fruits of the Crystal Palace.

7 The Building Goes Up

To a generation which found the first, faint gas-light almost unbearably brilliant, railway speeds of 40 m.p.h. or so breathtaking and the electric telegraph an impenetrable and probably sinister mystery, the erection of the Crystal Palace was something to wonder at. The first column went up on 26 September 1850, and thereafter the building grew like a mushroom thanks to the pains Fox and Henderson had taken to ensure the accuracy of the standardized parts, thanks to their lightness (only the nave trusses weighed more than a ton) and thanks to the preliminary work and organization which ensured a steady supply of material, and its swift transportation from the Midlands to Euston by the London and North-Western railway. From the terminus to Hyde Park and back Pickfords' pair-horse wagons plied to and fro in a steady stream.

The columns are usually described as octagonal, which is not strictly accurate but no precise term exists to describe a figure composed of four flat surfaces alternating with four part-cylindrical ones. The base-plates below the foundation sockets varied from 1 ft. × 2 ft. to 3 ft. × 2 ft. according to location and load to be carried, just as the columns themselves varied in wall thickness from $\frac{3}{8}$ in. to $1\frac{1}{4}$ in. according to load. All the columns were 8 in. in outside diameter,

18 ft. 8 in. long to which was added a 'connecting' piece of 3 ft. 4½ in. length. These connecting pieces were secured to the flanges by 1 in. Whitworth bolts and each had one, two, three or four opposing pairs (at top and bottom) of wide projecting ribs or wings cast with suitable 'snugs' to locate the cross girders correctly in relation to the bolt-holes. According to their positions in the three-tier, two-tier or single-tier parts of the building the connecting pieces carried either another column, with yet another connecting piece and column on top of that, or simple capping plates for the single-tier columns.

The construction was started from the middle of the building and worked outwards in two rows at a time. The connecting pieces were attached to the columns before these were raised by a pair of sheerlegs, dropped into the sockets (with thin canvas soaked in white lead interposed to make

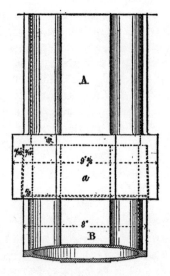

The column is of cast iron, cast hollow, and cylindrical on the interior. On the exterior it has four flat and four part-cylindrical faces. The upper portion of the column A is formed with a socket *a*, which is turned out slightly conical, and rests on the turned top of the lower part of the column B

a water-tight joint), and the bolts run home and tightened. In the words of the *Official Popular Guide* :

> ... so soon as two columns with their connecting pieces were fixed, a girder was run up, slipped between the projections of the connecting pieces and secured in place. An opposite pair of columns having been similarly elevated, another girder was attached to them; and thus two sides of a square were formed, and maintained in a vertical position by poles acting as supports to them. Two other girders being then hoisted, and slipped between the connecting pieces on the remaining two sides of the square, a rigid table was constructed. The 'shores' or supports were then removed, together with the sheerlegs, and the whole apparatus was at liberty, for the purpose of recommencing a similar operation in an adjoining 24-foot bay.
>
> When a sufficient number of these bays had been completed (starting from the intersection of the nave and transept) to warrant the addition, the hoisting of the columns for the first floor was commenced; more lofty sheerlegs being of course employed. The extension of the ground floor proceeding, as that of the first floor was carried on, a base was in turn afforded for the columns of the third tier; and thus the iron framework of the whole building rose ... without involving the necessity of any scaffolding whatever.

The fact that the columns were not perpendicular, because of the slight slope of the building from east to west, already referred to, was no more apparent to the naked eye than that one end of the apparently-level building was six feet higher than the other. One thing the human eye did take in approvingly was that each girder, as it was removed by crane from the cart, was placed first on a weighing machine to check the class of load it was to take, and then moved to an arrangement of Bramah hydraulic rams for strength-testing.

73

William Cubitt superintended the work on behalf of the Commissioners, and Charles Fox was almost daily on the site for upwards of fourteen hours a day. Joseph Paxton was also much in evidence and on 1 October he saw three columns and two girders put up and bolted in sixteen minutes. There was then a hold up as the fourth column for the square was found to be of the wrong calibre, but as the workmen grew more practised it was not uncommon for a complete square to be put up in twenty minutes. At strategic points of stress the columns were braced with diagonal tie-bars, bolted to top and bottom of the columns and meeting at the intersection of the X they formed in an ornamental device which concealed tensioning screws to tighten the bracing bars to their work.

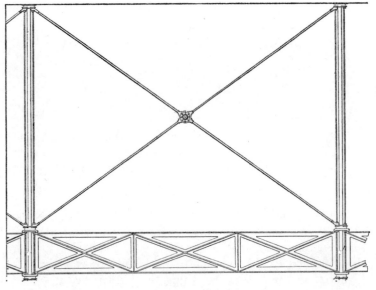

The diagonal bracing

Even at five shillings a time there was, as we have seen, no lack of spectators to watch the slender-looking cast-iron cobweb grow daily bigger. Prince Albert was often on the

74

scene, the Queen less often, and the workmen found themselves not infrequently under the eye of the best-known
figure in London—the Duke of Wellington.

The Duke was under no illusion about the Exhibition and
he did not share Prince Albert's high-minded hopes that it
would elevate taste, and bind together a brotherhood of men
who would set to beating their swords into ploughshares. As
he wrote soon after the opening: 'Whether the Shew will
ever be of any use to anybody may be questioned, but of
this I am certain nothing can be more successful.' Before this,
however, he had a small part to play in the success and, as
Ranger of Hyde Park, one of his duties in connection with
the building was to rid the Park of a 'squatter', a Mrs Hicks,
who had established herself in a little cabin in a hollow near
the 'Serpentine River' as it was still called, from which she
sold cakes and spring water. She had become almost an
institution but it was decided she had to go and, as always
when there was something to be done, the unpleasant duty
of turning her out was to fall on the Duke. He was nearly
eighty-two, very deaf, tortured with rheumatism and very
tired. Those who watched his progresses to and from the
Horseguards, to discharge his endless duties as Commander-
in-Chief, were alarmed to see that he not infrequently fell
asleep in the saddle. Even more distressing to those who
watched, discreetly out of sight, were his struggles to dis-
mount and worse struggles to remount: but they knew
better than to offer help. He might be growing frail but there
was duty to be done, and the subject of the Hyde Park
squatter crops up often in his inimitable letters. He wrote
almost daily to Lady Salisbury and reported:

> *October 13th* ... However she became established, I
> entertain no doubt that it will be a troublesome job to
> remove her! and I have determined that I will go to
> work regularly.
> *October 15th* When Sir Harry Smith was in England
> a year or two ago, he reminded me of my old Practice
> with the Army.

When there was any difficulty and they came to me to report it, and to ask what they should do, my answer was, 'I will get upon my Horse and take a look; and then tell you!' Accordingly, as soon as I shall reach my own house tomorrow, I will get upon my Horse and take a look at this squatter! and I think that I shall have no difficulty in pointing out the mode of settling that one!

November 4th It is very true that it is not fair to lay upon my shoulders all the unpopularity of the measures for clearing out the parks preparatory to the Grand Shew in 1851. But I am afraid it is never unfair to work the willing horse! I am always ready to go; and therefore I am always in harness.

November 15th I have the pleasure of informing you we have got rid of the Squatter in the Park. She has quitted her Residence, which has been pulled down and the ground on which it stood or rather fell has been levelled....

What the Duke did not tell Lady Salisbury was that Mrs Hicks received ten guineas compensation, to which she had no legal right, for the loss of her 'Residence' and that those guineas came from the Duke's pocket. The Duke's frequent visits to the building as it went up were invariably met with cheers from the workmen and visitors, equally invariably acknowledged with one finger raised to the hat brim and no change of countenance. The hisses, boos and brickbats of 1831, when he opposed the Reform Bill, were forgotten (not by the Duke, however), and cheers were no novelty to him. Another recipient of cheers was Prince Albert whose small stock of popularity now began to grow as public enthusiasm for his Exhibition mounted. At least, the *Illustrated London News* published an engraving of the Prince in his carriage on the Exhibition site captioned: 'Prince Albert being loudly cheered by the workmen when he left after a visit to the site.' Unfortunately the picture included another vehicle and the caption rather tactlessly continued: 'Entering the gates is a dray with 250 gallons of beer for the men.'

As the framework of the building grew, more doubts began to be cast on its strength, despite the hydraulic testing of every girder as it came on the site. Those serried ranks of slender columns and the delicate-seeming tracery of the X-formation trusses must have appeared alarmingly slight to eyes accustomed to masonry and brick. Particular fears were expressed about the galleries. One of the expensive additions to the original plan, apart from the semi-circular transept, was a second series of galleries running almost around the full length of the outer walls of the second tier. The originally planned galleries were 'free standing'. With the second series included the galleries stretched for a mile and three-quarters and added five acres to the eighteen acres of ground-floor space. Surely all these acres of gallery, loaded with exhibits and people could not be carried on such cobwebby girders?

To set fears at rest the contractors staged a demonstration in front of the Queen and Prince, their three eldest children, many of the Commissioners, journalists and as many of the public as were there to watch. A length of gallery was erected on the ground, standing on suitable blocks so that the girders were visibly taking the load just as though they were raised to column height. The demonstration started with three hundred workmen jumping up and down until they were breathless; trolleys laden with cannon balls were trundled to and fro, then a corps of the Royal Engineers were marched, counter-marched, quick-marched and marked time in quick time and finally Mr Fox undertook to drive a railway locomotive along the length of gallery. Fortunately, however, nobody thought this was necessary after what they had seen, which is probably just as well as no locomotive was at hand.

Until the building was far enough advanced for the glaziers to start work one of the sights which attracted the visitors was the wood-working machinery. As we have seen, wood and iron would have been interchangeable in many vital parts of the building (apart from the floors), and the pressure of time was responsible for the choice of wood for some parts which would have been better in metal, preferably galvanized, as experience was to prove. The maintenance and painting of the roofing timbers, for example, was a crippling expense in later years; but in 1850 nobody foresaw that the building designed for six months' use would stand for eighty-five years before it was destroyed by fire—in the woodwork.

Shortage of time therefore dictated the use of wood for the main gutters, Paxton gutters, ridge beams, transept ribs and many miles of glazing bars, to say nothing of the lead-covered cat-walks behind the ornamental parapets and many other parts. Many of these items were of quite complex shapes, particularly the glazing bars and ridges, and to have milled these from metal castings or drawn billets would have been a fairly slow process by the techniques of 1850. Multiple-head milling or routing cutters for woodwork were well advanced, though, and it is worth remembering that mass-production started with the elder Brunel's ingenious automatic machines for making pulley blocks for the Royal Navy during the Napoleonic War. The Navy's demand for blocks was far outstripping the traditional blockmakers' ability to supply, and Brunel's machinery not only saved the day but turned out better blocks than those made by hand.

It was certainly fascinating to the visitors to see planks being fed into the machines and emerging as several parallel lengths of ridge, sash-bar or gutter, grooved, rebated, bevelled, ridged and fluted all in a single pass. Even the circular saw which faced-off the Paxton gutters into their 24 ft. lengths was combined with a quadrantal cutter which simultaneously shaped the ends so that when two lengths were placed together there was the chamfered drainage hole to let out the water. Power-driven drills (or augers as they were still called) working in jig-frames bored all the necessary holes of appropriate diameters at suitable angles to the required depths to take the galvanized nails which held all the roofing materials together; therefore no time was lost in assembly as, like the columns and girders, everything was accurately shaped and machined ready to drop into place.

After leaving the shaping machines the lengths of wood-work were dipped into successive long, narrow troughs filled with primer and paint, on leaving which they passed through jigs which held suitable bristle-pads at strategic angles to brush off the surplus paint. This 'machine painting', as it was called, was also quite new, and after leaving the brushing jigs the lengths were hung on suitable racks to dry. Before the glass went in, the part of the building where all this work was done was kept dry by canvas covers stretched over the framing. The gallery rails, and the balustrades to twelve pairs of staircases, were capped by more than two miles of stout mahogany rail $2\frac{1}{4}$ in. in diameter with a 1 in. flat on the underside. This hand rail was also formed in one pass from roughly squared lengths of mahogany in another multiple-cutter machine. All the machinery was designed in detail, much of it from Paxton's rough drawings, by Edward Cowper, one of Fox and Henderson's employees who later set up in business on his own.

By November 1850 *Punch*'s name of 'Crystal Palace' coupled with the incredibly rapid growth of the framework, captured the public imagination. The voices of opposition began to be muted, but some of the objections were based on fears which had to be taken seriously. One of these fears, justified enough in view of the ultimate fate of the building, was of fire. Paxton explained that a 24 in. main was being laid from Chelsea Waterworks, and that this would supply enough water to throw a column 70 ft. high: twenty-five fire points were to be established in the building, each with a hydrant, a manual pumping engine on wheels and the necessary appurtenances of hoses, buckets and so forth. There were to be seventeen unobstructed exits, always open but guarded against unauthorized entry by one-way turnstiles.

Ten weeks after the first column was raised the building was far enough advanced for the first pair of transept ribs to be hoisted into place. As with everything else of importance this was supervised by Charles Fox helped, on this occasion, by both Henderson and Paxton. Including the lead-covered timber 'flats' at either side the transept arch spanned 72 ft. with just over 60 ft. clear at the interior base. It was supported directly upon the columns except at the 72 ft. intersection of nave and transept where it was supported on the wrought-iron nave trusses. The curved ribs, stayed and braced with an ingenious linkage of adjustable diagonal tie-bars, were the only large structural members of wood. They were marked out, cut and assembled on the site, and like all composite curved structures they were a good deal more complicated than they seemed.

All the horizontal girders of the framework were hoisted by horse power; by using a snatch-block anchored to the ground between the sheerlegs one horse, or a pair for the heavier members, could give a straight-line pull and raise the girder to the required height just as quickly as a modern crane. More elaborate means were needed for the transept ribs which would doubtless now be raised by a giant mobile tower crane.

The ribs were fastened together temporarily in pairs by suitable spars and as the width of the ribs was greater than the clear space between girders it was necessary to juggle them through the gap with one side higher than the other. Four pairs of sheerlegs were rigged up on the roof girders at the appropriate places, with four sets of ropes passing through compound pulley blocks and snatch blocks to four strategically placed geared winches. Using a speaking trumpet, Fox directed the men on the winches to hoist, stay or back off as necessary until the lower edge of the pair of ribs was high enough to back off and lower on to planks placed on rollers. The elevated higher side of the ribs was then similarly lowered on to more planks and rollers, and once the hoisting ropes were cast off the rollers allowed the ribs to be easily moved a few inches to and fro until they were located over their columns: screw jacks were then used to raise the ribs, whilst the planks were removed, and then lower them into place. By comparison with the use of a large crane it was a tedious operation, but straightforward enough and all the ribs were in place inside a week, where-upon the work of glazing the roof began.

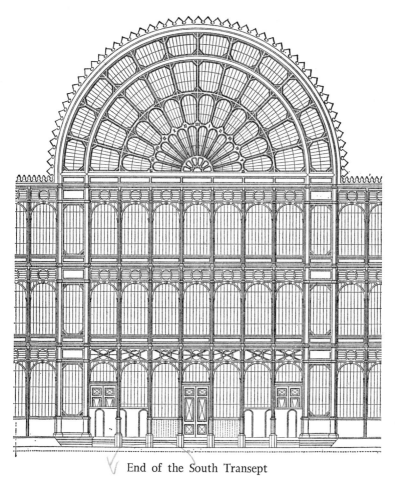

End of the South Transept

The external transept-ends were like giant fan-lights formed of gracefully curved cast-iron segments bolted together. Eleven 'sticks' to the fan divided the semi-circle into twelve radial segments and a little-known detail, seldom shown in the contemporary prints, is that on the south face of the building the lower circumferential borders of these segments were numbered in Roman numerals from VI on the viewer's left, to XII at the top, and from I to VI again on the viewer's right. A 24 ft. long double-ended hand indicated the daylight hours clearly enough as the operative half of the hand showed up well against the glazed areas of the sector, but the inoperative end was less conspicuous against the panelled area below the semi-circle. A second, less important, double-ended hand, 16 ft. in length, indicated the minutes over a similar sector on the smallest segment of the fan-light, whilst two conventional 5 ft. diameter dials were attached to the gallery rails inside the building.

Owen Jones, who was responsible for the decoration of the building, helped devise the external dial with its blue numerals on a white ground; the hands were of gilded copper.

This ingenious timepiece was the world's first large-scale, practicable electric master-and-slave clock system, the fore-runner of the modern Synchronome, and it was devised by William Shepherd. The power came from six small primary batteries energizing eight electro-magnets; these gave im-pulse to the pendulum which, in turn, drove the wheel-work of the clock train. By a clever spring remontoire mechanism the impulse given to the pendulum was constant irrespective of variations in the battery current. The internal slave dials were worked electro-magnetically just as their modern counterparts are and the whole concept was in advance of its time, particularly when it is remembered that Alexander Bain's patent for the first workable electric clock was only taken out nine years earlier.

Truth compels the admission that there were occasions when Shepherd's electric mechanism could not cope with strong winds blowing across the face of the building, but it was one of the most admired features of the Exhibition. Its slow, sonorous hour-striking inspired Samuel Warren to immortalize it in a stanza in his apologue of the Crystal Palace, The Lily and the Bee:

Hark! A sound! Startling my soul!
A toll profound!
The hollow tongue of Time,
Telling its awful flight...

Glazing of the walls had begun before the transept ribs
were raised. This was a straightforward enough job, mostly
done from inside the building and therefore needing no
scaffolding. A point which is not always realized, as few
of the contemporary pictures make it clear, is that only
the second- and third-tier walls were fully glazed. The ground
floor had the same pattern of pillars 24 ft. apart with three
sections in each, and there were glazed areas flanking the
doors and in some other places, but most of the sections were
filled with tongued and grooved boards, painted off-white,
arranged vertically. As the boards were 12 in. wide their
vertical divisions matched those of the 10 in. wide glass
panes in their narrow vertical glazing bars. As the horizontal
glazing bars were narrower, the vertical emphasis of the
external columns and the wall glazing and boarding added
to the beauty of the building by giving necessary contrast
to the long horizontals of the shape. Modern plate glass in
sheets large enough to fill each 24 ft. module without inter-
mediate framing and glazing bars would not have nearly so
happy an effect.

The glazing of the roof was a fascinating business which
attracted a lot of attention. As already stated the 'flat' roofs
were composed of a series of ridges and valleys, 8 ft. apart,
with the patent Paxton gutters supporting the lower ends
of the panes and discharging the rainwater and condensate
from them at 24 ft. intervals into main gutters running along
the longitudinal girders. As the whole building sloped longi-
tudinally 1 in. in 24 ft. from west to east, there was nothing
to hinder the flow of water in the main gutters; but as the
building was level from south to north the Paxton gutters,
following the south-north axis, had to be bowed upwards so
that the centre of each was 2½ in. higher than the ends.
This was done by an arrangement of cast-iron shoes let into

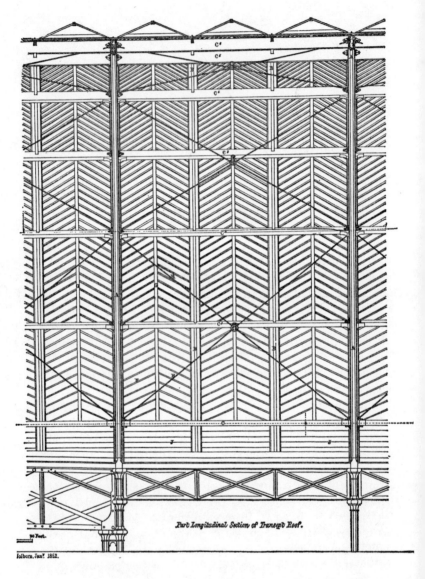

Part Longitudinal Section of Transept Roof.

30 Feet.

Tolborn, Jan.ʸ 1852.

A longitudinal section of a portion of the roof

rebates cut into the underside of each end of a gutter from which a tie rod ran under iron struts placed 4 ft. either side of the centre; adjusting nuts at each end of the tie rod could be screwed up until the necessary camber had been put into the gutter. At intervals the gutters ran above the transverse wooden roof trusses, and these gutters were more simply bowed by the interposition of suitable vertical struts wedged between truss and gutter. At the ends of the roofs where they abutted against the vertical wall rising from the second and third tiers, or terminated in triangular vertical faces, the Paxton gutters were made with only one side groove and with the opposite face sawn and planed flat.

The bevelled edges of the gutters on which the glass rested were dovetail-slotted at suitable intervals to receive the glazing bars, which were 1 in. wide by 1⅜ in. deep, with a groove on either side 3/16 in. wide and 5/16 in. deep to take the glass. Three glazing bars in every 24 ft. length were of larger section, 2½ in., to support the ridge beam during the initial process of assembly.

The ridges and valleys of the roofing were not carried to the outer edges of the building where room was left for a catwalk or lead-covered 'flat'. This and the ridge and valley roofs themselves were hidden from ground level view by a frilly parapet or cornice made of sheet zinc interspersed with cast-iron finials. Similar cornices ran round the ends of the semi-circular transept roof concealing from a frontal view that the barrel roof was also glazed in the ridge and valley manner, with the important difference (apart from the ridges having to be curved), that the glazing bars ran diagonally downwards from ridge to valley with the panes cut to correspond. This arrangement prevented rainwater from lying against the bars and possibly finding its way through weak places in the putty. The outer surfaces of the curved ribs were shaped in the same fashion as the Paxton gutters and consequently served both to carry the weight of the vaulted roof and to carry away rain and condensate.

It is difficult to improve on the contractors' own description of the glazing process:

The roof is glazed in the following manner: a number of sash-bars are prepared with the grooves filled with putty, and the ridge piece is raised up and supported by the broad sash-bars [which were not nailed down at this stage].

A sheet of glass is then pushed into the groove of one of these broad sash-bars, and another bar is then pressed upon its edge and brought into its slot and secured by a nail at each end. [The nail holes, slightly undersize, having been previously drilled at the correct angles there was little risk of cracking the pane.] The sheet of glass is then pushed up into the groove in the ridge, and the putty is smoothed with a knife. Another pane is then inserted, and so on until the workman arrives at the next broad bar which he lifts out of its place and introduces the pane of glass as before, the ridge being supported in the meantime by the narrow bars already inserted. A provision is made, however, by which the glass can be introduced without removing the sash-bar, which is particularly useful in case of a pane being accidentally broken after the glazing is complete. It will be seen that the fillet is partially removed on one side of each bar [the leading edge being cut back 1/16 in.], so that if one edge of the glass be slipped into the groove in the next bar, its other edge can be brought down past the reduced fillet on to the shoulder; the glass is then slipped sideways a little so as to enter the groove, and it is thus secured at both sides.

This method of glazing with these grooved sash-bars has been proved by many years experience at Chatsworth ... to be much superior to the ordinary method of fixing the glass on bars with a simple shoulder on each side A smaller quantity of putty is used and, being confined in the groove, it is not liable to crack and break away.

This modestly leaves out of account one feature of the

roof-glazing procedure which most caught the public fancy. This was that the bulk of the work was not done by men standing on planks athwart the girders but from wheeled trolleys which ran to and fro using the Paxton gutters as railways. Each trolley carried two men and a boy, and an opening in the centre allowed supplies of glass, putty and bars to be passed to the men from below. Curved iron stays supported canvas covers which enabled the work to be carried on in wet weather. These trolleys were also used on the transept along the top of which another cat-walk ran, and with suitable block and tackle anchored to this the men on the trolleys could lower themselves down the slopes, slipping in the panes of glass as they went almost as quickly as they could on the level. According to the *Official Popular Guide* these trolleys materially helped eighty glaziers to put in 18,000 panes, covering 62,600 ft. superficial, in a single week.

On the flat roofs the trolleys worked outwards towards the edges of the building, with the crews necessarily riding backwards and fixing the bars and panes behind them as they went. Having reached the cat-walk the trolley was light enough to be up-ended, manoeuvred sideways and lowered on to the next pair of gutters leaving the 8 ft. space it had just vacated to be glazed by men standing on planks straddling the supporting girders.

The little covered wagons silhouetted against the winter sky as they crept about the highest girders, leaving trails of glass behind them, naturally attracted the visitors and were judged worthy of attention from the *Illustrated London News* artist, whose picture of the process makes one regret again the absence of high-speed photography in 1850. Never could such implausible little wheels have supported the weight of two men and a boy and a load of glass in gutters of such strange shapes; nor could so flimsy a ridge have supported panes of cobweb let alone of glass. Some other contemporary views of the finished roofing also give the impression that the panes were put in without glazing bars to hold them and to seal the joints.

As the glazing work neared completion in January 1851, and the great Palace, with its swarms of workmen, glittered in the wintry sunlight public enthusiasm for it grew apace; particularly when it became known that the admission charges (apart from season-ticket holders) were to range from one shilling to one pound, with forty times more shilling than pound days. Prince Albert's 'Great Shew', as Wellington called it, was not to be just for the nobs but something all but the poorest could enjoy.

The plaudits were still not enough to silence opposition completely, and although a very severe gale in January partly lifted a 72 ft. length of unfinished roof, but otherwise disproved the fears that Sir George Airey held about the building's stability, new objections were raised. Colonel Sibthorp was still loosing off cannonades against the influx of tawdry foreign goods, thieves, anarchists, assassins, secret societies, Mariolaters, who were all being encouraged to do their damnable worst in the name of 'the greatest trash, the greatest fraud, the greatest imposition ever foisted upon the people of England'. He now found another target in the building itself.

The Colonel had joined with those who had predicted the building would blow down in the first gale of wind or fall down under the weight of nineteen acres of snow. When neither of these things happened he spoke up in the House of Commons as the owner of a famous garden and an authority on glasshouses. Anybody, he said, who possessed a hot-house could have told the Prince that hot-houses were hot. The Crystal Palace was going to be infernally hot, a furnace, a sweat-box, a Turkish bath; in addition to being swindled, robbed and infected with bubonic plague or venereal disease anybody foolish enough to go would be sweltered to fever point, would take cold on coming out, chills would supervene leading to ague, pneumonia....

Without going quite so far as the Colonel in calling the Crystal Palace a death trap (as well as a Tower of Babel, a cave of Adullam and a hotbed of Popery) there were many others who feared the place would be too hot. Those nearer the project had complete faith, fully justified, in the ventilating system, but it was clear that there might be a problem from too much top light causing glare and discomfort on all but the dullest days. Early in the planning stage there had been talk of a series of calico blinds to be drawn horizontally under the flat roofs, but this idea was abandoned probably because it was thought to be impractical or unsightly—or both.

The whole area of ridge and valley roofing was in fact covered with white canvas, woven in yard-wide breadths. Two breadths sewn together and attached to two adjacent ridge beams hung down into the intervening valley so that the seam, suitably pierced with eyeletted drain holes, ran a few inches above the Paxton gutter. These canvas covers were not visible from ground level, and the splendid contemporary 'aeronautical' view of the palace does not show them. From inside they had the desired effect of cutting out glare and giving a pleasantly diffused top light throughout the building, except in the central intersection and along the length of the transept, as the barrel vault was left uncovered. It seems that few of the visitors to the Exhibition realized that the roof was covered in this way, although many remarked on the theatrical effect on unclouded days as shafts of sunlight poured through the transept roof and glittered on Osler's great glass fountain which made a fitting focal point in the middle of the great glass house.

It is said that the construction of one of London's Victorian theatres was well advanced before it was realized that the architect's drawings showed no staircase whereby the cash customers might reach the gallery. No such mistake was made with the Crystal Palace, which was adequately equipped with twelve pairs of staircases serving the two ranges of galleries. Except for being bolted together and therefore, like the rest of the building, easily dismantled they contained no unusual features and are best displayed in the Contractors' drawings and described in their own words:

... the staircases consist of two parallel flights 8 ft.

wide, with a space of 8 ft. between them, leading to
a landing 24 ft. long and 8 ft. wide, from opposite sides
of which two flights of stairs lead to the galleries. The
staircase is covered by a cross gallery, 48 ft. long and
24 ft. wide, which unites the two main galleries, and

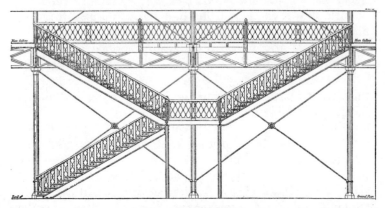

Section through Staircase

in which two spaces, or well-holes, of 8 ft. wide by 16 ft.
long are formed to receive the upper flights of stairs. By
this arrangement there are two passengers of 8 ft. wide
at every part. The above dimensions are given to explain
the manner in which two 24 ft. bays of the building are
divided out and occupied by a staircase. Owing to the
space occupied by the columns, balustrade etc. the
actual width from centre to centre of the strings is
7 ft. 1 in., and the actual clear width between balustrades is 6 ft. 10¼ in.

The landing is supported by eight small cast-iron
columns, of similar section to those which support the
building but of 5 in. diameter instead of 8 in.... Four
cast-iron strings of I-section are bolted to these columns
to carry the lower flights of stairs, and two similar
cast-iron strings are bolted to each girder at the sides
of the landing, and to cast-iron trellis girders under the

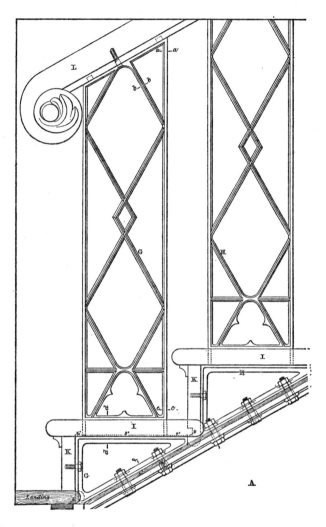

An elevation of the cast-iron string for the upper flights of stairs, showing also a section of the same, and a portion of the stairs and balustrade

gallery floor for carrying the upper flights. The vertical
struts of these trellis girders, which are of the strongest
section, are widened to receive the strings which rest
upon projecting snugs cast upon the girders, to which
they are each secured by four bolts and nuts. A series
of standards, with open triangular frames at bottom,
are bolted on the upper edges of the strings, for the
purpose of receiving the treads and risers of the stairs
[and simultaneously forming the open cast-iron balus-
trading]. There are twenty-one stairs in each flight. The
columns on each side of a staircase are strengthened
by diagonal bracing in both tiers, and the strings of the
staircase also form strong diagonal struts. . . .

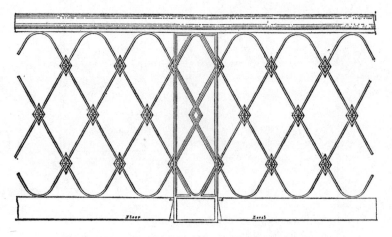

An elevation of the lower part of the gallery front

It might have been supposed that Fox and Henderson
would have taken advantage of their iron-mastery to make
open cast-iron treads for the stairways, but they were probably deterred by fear of accidents should the iron become
polished with use. Treads and risers therefore were of elm,
the former a generous 1 ft. 2 in. wide and the latter a gentle
7½ in. high, making a fairly shallow, easy rise.

One of the less happy features of fashionable modern architecture is the use of two or three wide planks, fixed to similar wide uprights, to make staircase and landing rails and balustrades. Except in a few exterior applications where a sort of glorified paddock fence is not inappropriate, these balustrades are as unsightly as they are wasteful of good timber. By contrast the Crystal Palace balustrades and gallery rails were light and elegant. As noted, the balustrade standards were cast integrally, one to each step, with the triangular sections supporting the treads which were slotted into place. The gallery railing, of rather similar pattern, was cast in short lengths with the ornamental diamond-shaped bosses concealing a kind of hook and eye arrangement by means of which they were quickly latched together.

By the end of the year 1850, twenty-two weeks after Fox and Henderson took possession of the site, the building was finished in the sense that it was up and almost completely glazed with its galleries, staircases and floors in place. The rate of building had been not far short of an acre a week and so far everything had gone without a hitch; but there was an immense amount to do in the sixteen weeks to opening day, and the fact that exhibits began to arrive in February hindered the work of fitting-out.

The work to be done included laying on water and gas, installing the lavatories and fire points, building entrance halls, reception counters, a retiring room for the Queen, three restaurants, a large lecture room, administrative offices and a small boiler room near the north-west corner to supply steam and hot water to the restaurants. A larger boiler room, quite apart from the main building, contained three Armstrong boilers to supply live steam to the 'machinery in motion' exhibits.

In so light a building there was little need for artificial light, but sufficient gas-lamps had to be installed to allow the police who patrolled the building at night to see what they were doing. Railings and gates had to be put up round the entire site of twenty-six acres, *and* nearly everything had to be painted. The glazing bars and frames had been painted

93

before they were put up, as we have seen. Although there is no direct evidence it is tolerably certain that the outermost rectangle of columns and their connecting pieces, the outer faces of which were, of course, visible from outside the building and some other parts of the external walls were also painted before erection. This still left a prodigious amount of iron work, much of it of a rather finicking nature, to paint by hand; and to paint moreover in four colours.

Owen Jones was the man responsible for the decoration. He was known as Alhambra Jones because of his enthusiasm for Moorish art and architecture, and his colour scheme met with almost universal disapproval when it was announced and almost total approbation when the result was seen. The colours were white, red, Cambridge blue and a fairly strong yellow. Most of the components had more than one colour which added delicate 'picking out' to the labour. The general scheme was that most of the vertical wooden surfaces, the glazing bars and so forth, were white; other vertical flat surfaces were blue but convex or concave surfaces were yellow. The columns therefore presented alternate blue and yellow faces. All the horizontal surfaces visible from below, the girder flanges for example, were red but the vertical parts were blue again, with the diagonal parts of the lattice girders picked out in white. The exterior paintwork was mainly white or off-white, again with blue picking out the circular faces of the external columns and the reveals.

Owen Jones was also responsible for the design of the light and elegant railings all round the building. With the scares of anarchists, foreign secret societies and assassins in mind one body of the Commissioners were for enclosing the whole site with a high fortress-like palisade, and it was seriously proposed at one stage to bring over a body of French plainclothes police to keep an eye open for would-be revolutionaries from the Continent. Fortunately wiser counsels prevailed and in his letters to his foreign correspondents Prince Albert poured particular scorn on this proposal. In the event it was found that a relatively small body of uniformed London policemen and Mr Owen Jones's ornamental railings were quite enough.

The effect of the colour scheme was certainly pleasing, and was complemented by the hanging banners which divided sections and announced the countries and classes of exhibits: they were red with white borders and lettering. Less pleasing, to the Commissioners, was the delay in getting the work done. It was the first setback in an operation which had gone forward without a hitch. Iron straps of special shape were made to hook over the girders and trusses, and scaffold poles were lashed to these to support what the *Official Popular Guide* called 'a perfect cloud of boards', but despite this elaborate staging all the paint had to be applied by hand and the work lagged.

Henry Cole was particularly perturbed as upon him had fallen the inconspicuous but essential job of marshalling and co-ordinating the flow of exhibits. Matthew Digby Wyatt, Secretary of the Executive Committee, was nominally responsible and also worked like a Trojan, but most of the tedious detail work was done by Cole. When it is considered that 7,381 British and 6,556 foreign exhibitors were involved it can be seen that it was no easy task, particularly as many of the foreign exhibitors courteously tried but signally failed to make their intentions clear in the sort of English exemplified on one consignment which was prominently labelled to:

> *Sir Vyatt & Sir Fox Enderson Esquire,*
> *Grate Ezposition Park of Hide at London.*
> GLACE SOFTLY TO BE POSED UPRIGHTLY

The building was opened for the reception of goods on 12 February, but the painters had scarcely started aloft. Everybody at work below was at hazard from paint splashes, large areas of the floor, below the painters, had to be kept covered and the exhibits had to be kept in their packing cases or covered with dust sheets which were at a premium. Cole's notes recorded the state of affairs:

The delays in painting alarmed us. On the 27th February, it appeared obvious that the painting would not be completed by the 1st of May. Colonel Reid [Chairman of Executive Committee] with Mrs Reid came, and I called the Colonel's attention to the slow progress of the painting. Mrs Reid valiantly urged her husband to recommend that an extra £1,000 should be offered to Fox & Henderson for speed. I found out from Mr Fox that he could and would hasten the work if paid £1,000 extra. Lord Granville and Mr Cubitt agreed that he should be tempted by the bribe. Mr Fox hastened the work, but I am happy to record flinched from taking the money, and afterwards told me that he could not take it. On the 20th of March, the painters were vigorously at work and with plenty of scaffolding. Again I note, 7th of April painting and removal of staging very behind-hand; wrote to Fox and Henderson and told Mr Fox that the painters must be out by the 14th of April, or the Sappers would enter, take away the scaffolding, and turn the men out. 12th April I wrote 'scaffolding not yet out', but it was all down well before the 30th April.

It seems a little unfair to refer to the extra £1,000 offered to, but not accepted by, Fox & Henderson as a bribe. They had taken great financial risks and worked wonders to put the great building up so quickly, and although the painting work did run behind time the whole interior was finished before opening day, and the exterior nearly finished. Fox and Henderson had nearly five hundred painters at work at one time, and it would not have been physically possible to accommodate more.

Quite apart from the cost of wages for extra painters, it seems that Fox & Henderson had exceeded their estimate as the extra range of galleries and the transept were very expensive. The available figures are contradictory. The Stationery Office's *Commemorative Album*, compiled in 1950 by C. H. Gibbs-Smith to mark the centenary, quotes figures from the Commissioners' records which give the total expenditure as '£355,742, including the building and fittings at approximately £170,000'. The 'approximate' sum for the building fits the original estimate suspiciously well and the Commissioners may have wished to conceal that the total included some extras allowed to Fox & Henderson to meet their extra expenditure. It seems fair to leave the last word with the contractors who recorded:

> ... the formal contract was not executed until the 31st of October, 1850; but the contractors had begun to fix the columns on the 26th of September, and had already incurred liabilities to the extent of £50,000. The tender for the original design was £79,800 for the use of the building or £150,000 for the complete purchase of it, but an additional piece of 936 ft. long and 48 ft. wide was added to the north side, and various other additions were made. The cost of erecting the building in the short space of time allowed for it also considerably exceeded expectation, so that the actual prime cost of the building amounted to about £200,000 or about £25 per 100 square feet of ground covered.

Of the fitting-out work in general there is not much to be said, as it was a matter of straightforward plumbing, carpentry, and the thousand and one other chores attendant upon finishing and furnishing a house on a gargantuan scale. That it all *was* done, with the exception of some of the exterior painting, in fifteen weeks is as remarkable as the erection of the bare building in twenty-two weeks.

According to popular belief one last difficulty threatened the Crystal Palace. The threat came from the elm trees and could perhaps be seen as Colonel Sibthorp's revenge. The few small elms near the northern end of the building rose through one of the restaurants and had their heads outside the glass roof (in the single tier of the building), as the boles passed through close-fitting voids made for the purpose. In the great transept, however, the arched glass roof passed a few feet above the crowns of the three fine fully grown trees.

As March and April came so did the sparrows in their hundreds to nest in this nice warm retreat. Where formerly those below had been at risk from paint splashes now they, and the exhibits being marshalled into place, were exposed to aerial bombardment of a different kind. According to Christopher Hobhouse even the Prince was not spared, and all the ingenuity of Paxton, Cole, Fox and the rest could not find a solution. Even governmental cerebration could not suggest a remedy and the Prime Minister, Lord John Russell, had to be reminded that a glasshouse is not the best place in which to discharge shot-guns.

In despair, it is said, Prince Albert was obliged to tell the Queen why he had recently discouraged her from accompanying him on his visits of inspection. In despair the Queen did what her predecessors and their governments had done for half a century. She sent for the Duke, and steeled herself to overcome modesty enough to adumbrate the awful dilemma in tones loud enough to penetrate the ducal deafness. Without hesitation the Duke of Wellington considered the problem, found the correct solution and propounded the remedy in four words: 'Try sparrow hawks, Ma'am.' According to Lord Playfair,* at the mere sight of the Duke of Wellington and the words 'sparrow hawks', 'the sparrows flew out of the Crystal Palace in a body and were never seen again.'

There are times when myth becomes so firmly entrenched that it seems almost the act of a vandal to question it; but, alas! truth demands the admission that no reliable evidence exists to support this charming story of the Duke's last great service to his country. Lord Playfair's account seems convincing until it is discovered that his *Memoirs*, from which it is taken, were not compiled for him (by Sir Thomas Wemyss Reid), until fifty years after the event, and include the admission that the story was 'filched' from a provincial journal. The Duke's own correspondence of the time, so replete with references to the Crystal Palace, says nothing

*Better known as Dr (or Sir) B. Lyon Playfair the eminent scientist: raised to the peerage 1892.

of sparrows and sparrow hawks. Above all, the Queen's voluminous and brilliantly observant *Journal* does not mention the problem, although her enthusiasm for her beloved Albert's masterpiece, as she saw it, led her into even more minute detail than usual. It is sadly true that after the Queen died her youngest daughter, Princess Beatrice, her literary executor, went through her mother's Journals transcribing from each page what she thought the Queen would have thought fit for the public eye, and dropping the original pages one by one, as she transcribed them, into the fire. Though strait-laced neither Queen nor Princess was so prudish as to suppress so mildly indelicate a story, and its absence from the *Journal* is strong evidence that it is only a myth.

Perhaps the best verdict was given by Lady Longford, biographer of both the Queen and the Duke. She concluded that the story is apocryphal in fact but true to the spirit of the Duke who reached the end of his life as the Victorian age, exemplified in the Crystal Palace, reached its apogee.

8 High Noon in Hyde Park

This chapter heading is taken, with grateful acknowledgement, from L. T. C. Rolt's book, *Victorian Engineering*, and aptly sums up the triumphant success of the Great Exhibition. Although the Victorian age had forty more years to run, and the British Empire almost doubled in size in the years following the Exhibition, 1851 really does mark the high point when the nation's self-confidence was as yet unshaken by the Crimean War and other humiliating revelations, and when no Englishman would have admitted the possibility that other nations might one day equal, let alone surpass, Great Britain. Eighteen fifty-one was also the mid-point of Prince Albert's career as the unacknowledged, uncrowned king who had unobtrusively but firmly modernized the monarchy, and so indelibly impressed his principles upon the Queen that forty years later every problem she considered from the minor peccadilloes of a great-grandchild to the choice of a Viceroy of India had to be analysed on the basis of what *he* would have said, done or wished.

/As the opening day drew near opposition to the Exhibition dwindled further, but old and new objections cropped up and had to be answered. The building having demonstrated its ability to withstand gales and rain, a new scare was put about that when the Royal Salute was fired at the Queen's entrance the glass would shatter and make mincemeat of the notabilities assembled for the opening. The Queen recorded in her *Journal:*

> Everyone is occupied with the great day ... and my poor Albert is terribly fagged. All day and every day some question or other or some difficulty, *all* of which my beloved one takes with the greatest quiet and good humour.

Old cynics like the Duke of Wellington might say that the Exhibition would be no more than a raree-show of no lasting value, but in the end Prince Albert's hopes were fulfilled, at least in part, by the fact that the profits paid for the museums and institutes, now clustered round Exhibition Road, as well as scholarships and research grants. His unfulfilled hopes for a new era of peace and brotherhood were summed up in his address to the Commissioners:

> Gentlemen—the Exhibition of 1851 is to give us a true test and a living picture of the point of development at which the whole of mankind has arrived in the great task of making the laws of the Almighty man's standard of action, and a new starting point from which all nations will be able to direct their further exertions. I confidently hope the first impression which the view of this vast collection will produce upon the spectator will be that of deep thankfulness to the Almighty for the blessings which He has bestowed upon us already here below; and the second, the conviction that they can only be realized in proportion to the help which we are prepared to render to each other—therefore, only by peace, love and ready assistance, not only between individuals, but between the nations of the earth.

One of Prince Albert's hopes was that foreign visitors of influence would carry away some concept of the English form of constitutional monarchy and parliamentary government which made it possible to stage such a demonstration of wealth and co-operation at such a time. One of his dearest wishes was to see Prussia adopt the English form of constitution so as to make herself fit, in his eyes, to lead the German states into the united nation he longed to see.

The fact that Prussia did ultimately head the new German Empire, but only by making herself even more arbitrary and militaristic was a tragedy the Prince did not live to see. His letters and memoranda to King Frederick William IV of Prussia constantly urged the British form of government upon that mystical monarch who vacillated between a kind of milk-and-water benevolent feudalism and harsh autocracy. As Frederick William was elderly and tottering on the edge of the mental breakdown which overwhelmed him later, Prince Albert pinned greater hope upon his brother, who succeeded him as King William I of Prussia, and became the first Kaiser of the new Reich. The Prince hoped for a good attendance of notabilities and royalties for the opening, but succeeded in getting tentative acceptance only from Wilhelm, then known as the Prince of Prussia, and his wife and two children.* Consequently it was very galling to learn that the King of Prussia almost withdrew permission for his heir to attend because of scaremongering by the King of Hanover who wrote to him on 1 April:

> I hear that the Ministers as well as Prince Albert are beginning to jibber with anxiety over this rubbishy Exhibition in London. I beg of you, if you have time, to get read to you the speech of the most prominent and cleverest statesman we have, Lord Lyndhurst, a former Lord Chancellor, who gave a complete *exposé* in Parliament of the infamies, plots and *menées* of the excommunicated of all lands who are now in London. It is really a masterpiece, and not merely as a speech, but in the clearness with which he explained to the

* The elder of whom, Prince Frederick, married Victoria and Albert's firstborn, Princess Victoria, the Princess Royal, mother of Kaiser Wilhelm II.

Lords and Ministers how things are in London at the moment. I am not easily given to panicking, but I confess to you that I would not like anyone belonging to me exposed to the imminent perils of these times. Letters from London tell me that the Ministers will not allow the Queen and the great originator of this folly, Prince Albert, to be in London while the Exhibition is on, and I wonder at William wishing to go there with his son.

One reason why the old King of Hanover had been so unpopular in England was that he never learnt to curb his caustic tongue and, worse still, he was so often proved right. In this instance he was only partly right. The Government had not 'advised' the Queen and Prince to leave London whilst the Exhibition was on, but they had committed the folly of acquiescing in the Commission's arrangement for the opening ceremony, presided over by the Queen, to be a private affair for the benefit of the Commissioners themselves, their wives and friends, members of the Government and a few other dignitaries. This was an insult to the public in general, and the season-ticket holders in particular who had thought the expenditure of two or three guineas would entitle them to be present at the opening.

The decision was not announced until 19 April and the rather feeble excuse was that the Queen's nerves had not recovered from an attack on her in the previous June when a deranged half-pay officer named Robert Pate had struck her in the face with his walking stick. This was not the first attack on her, but the first actually to be physically harmful, and the Queen had certainly been shocked and distressed—largely because she had barely recovered from the birth of Prince Arthur. Eleven months had passed, though, and the excuse carried little weight. There were roars of protest headed by *The Times* which observed that the Queen was *not* Lady Godiva and then thundered:

What an unworthy part would these nervous advisers

cause the Queen of England to play! Surely Queen Victoria is not Tiberius or Louis XI, that she should be smuggled out of a great glass carriage into a great glass building under cover of the truncheons of the police and the broadswords of the Life Guards. Where most Englishmen are gathered together, there the Queen of England is most secure!

In the face of this and other onslaughts the Government, the Commissioners and the Court gave way, rather grudgingly it seems from reading between the lines of the Queen's journal, and it was made known just in time that the opening ceremony would be a full State affair with the public admitted; the public in this instance being those who could afford season tickets at their curiously discriminatory prices of three guineas for men and two for women. It is not clear whether this should be taken as a compliment or an insult to the 'female portion of the visitors' whose dresses, it will be remembered, made the provision of sweeping machines for the ground floor superfluous. In the event 25,605 season tickets were sold (13,494 men's and 12,111 women's), and it seems that nearly all the holders managed to be present at the opening, although undoubtedly a substantial minority were deterred by the prognostications of disaster.

Large crowds lined the route and assembled outside the building which, after early showers, began to sparkle in spring sunshine. At the time when work was started on the roof Sir Charles Barry had had the brilliant idea, which was carried out, of providing suitable sockets for short flag-poles, concealed behind the cornices of the flat roofs. On opening day and throughout the duration of the Exhibition the flags of all the nations, repeated again and again, fluttered from these thousand poles. The only disappointment to the waiting crowds was that the Queen drove in a closed landau and not in the great State Coach; but one experience of that conveyance on her Coronation Day had been enough for the Queen. Even her sailor uncle, King William IV, had declared it more nauseating than any ship he had served in, and another hundred years were to pass before modern technology controlled its sickening sway with concealed torsion bars and dampers.

The grand opening has been described often enough from the moment when the Crystal Palace did *not* fly asunder in lacerating fragments as the guns were fired; past the moment when revolutionaries did *not* seize the occasion to assassinate the Queen; on to the moment when Lord Granville was seen, bass broom in hand, sweeping shavings from the dais and the Lord Chancellor amused himself by turning the great crystal fountain on and off; on to the arrival of the royalties through the Coalbrookdale Gates; on to the state procession through the length of the building, with the Great Officers of the Household performing the difficult feat of looking dignified and at ease as they walked backwards; past the occasion when the procession was joined by a splendidly robed Chinese mandarin who turned out to be bogus; on to the swelling chorus of cheers for the royal family and those for the octogenarian Commander-in-Chief and the Master of the Ordnance (Wellington and Anglesey), arm-in-arm to support each other's hobbling (the Duke from rheumatism and the Marquess on the artificial leg which replaced the one blown off at Waterloo) and talking away in the penetrating tones of the very deaf loudly enough to be heard above the bellowing of Willis's great organ; on to the dais, which the Queen did mount, with the throne on which she did not sit; past the tedium of a long address from Prince Albert reiterating everything everybody knew about everything the Commission had done, past the lesser tedium of the Queen's short reply and on to the moment when the Exhibition was declared open, the royal party left and the 25,000 ticket-holders could begin to look about them.

The Queen's own description cannot be bettered; it runs to several thousand words and contains the following ecstatic passages:

> *May 1* This day is one of the greatest and most glorious days of our lives, with which to my pride and ⌐

joy the name of my dearly beloved Albert is for ever associated! We began the day with tenderest greetings and congratulations on the birth of our dear little Arthur.* He was brought in at breakfast and looked beautiful with blue ribbon on his frock. Mamma [the Duchess of Kent] and Victor [of Hohenlohe-Langenburg, husband of Queen Victoria's half-sister] were there, as well as all the children and our dear guests. Our little gifts of toys were added to by the *Pce.* and *Pcess.* [Prince and Princess of Prussia].

The Park presented a wonderful spectacle, crowds streaming through it—carriages and troops passing, quite like the Coronation and for *me* the same anxiety ... At ½ past 11 the whole procession in 9 state carriages was set in motion. Vicky and Bertie [Princess Royal and Prince of Wales] were in our carriage (the other children and Vivi [Princess Louise of Prussia, aged 12] did not go).... The Green Park and Hyde Park were one mass of densely crowded human beings, in the highest good humour and most enthusiastic. I never saw Hyde Park look as it did, being filled with crowds as far as the eye could reach. A little rain fell, just as we started, but before we neared the Crystal Palace, the sun shone and gleamed upon the gigantic edifice, upon which the flags of every nation were flying. We drove up Rotten Row and got out of our carriages at the entrance on that side. The glimpse through the iron gates of the transept, the waving palms and flowers, the myriads of people filling the galleries and seats around, together with the flourish of trumpets as we entered the building, gave a sensation I shall never forget and I felt much moved. We went for a moment into a little room where we left our cloaks and found Mamma and Mary [Princess Mary of Cambridge, wife of Duke of Teck, mother of Queen Mary]. ... In a few seconds we proceeded, Albert leading me, having Vicky at his hand

* Prince Arthur, later Duke of Connaught, born 1 May 1850 and named in honour of his godfather the Duke of Wellington.

and Bertie holding mine. The sight as we came to the centre where the steps and chair (on which I did *not* sit) was placed facing the beautiful crystal fountain was magic and impressive. The tremendous cheering, the joy expressed in every face, the *vastness* of the building, with all its decoration and exhibits, the sound of the organ (with 200 instruments and 600 voices, which yet seemed nothing) and my beloved husband, the creator of this peace festival 'uniting the industry and art of all nations', all this was indeed moving, and a day to live for ever. God bless my dearest Albert, and my dear country ... After the National Anthem had been sung, Albert left my side and at the head of the Commissioners—a curious assemblage of political and distinguished men—read the Report to me which is a long one, and I read a short answer. After this the Archbishop of Canterbury offered up a short and appropriate prayer, followed by the singing of Handel's Hallelujah Chorus, during which the Chinese Mandarin came forward and made his obeisance. ... The procession of great length began, which was beautifully arranged ... The nave was full of people, which had not been intended, and deafening cheers and waving hand-kerchiefs continued the whole time of our long walk from one end of the building to the other. One could of course see nothing but what was high up in the Nave and nothing in the Courts. The organs were but little heard, but the Military Band at one end had a fine effect, playing the march from *Athalie* as we passed along. The old Duke of Wellington and Ld Anglesey walked arm-in-arm, which was a touching sight .. We returned to our place and Albert told Lord Breadalbane to declare the Exhibition to be opened which he did in a loud voice saying 'Her Majesty commands me to declare this Exhibition open', when there was a flourish of trumpets followed by immense cheering. We then made our bow and left.

All these Commissioners and the Executive Committee etc. who had worked so hard and to whom such immense praise is due, seemed truly happy, and no one more so than Paxton, who may feel justly proud. He rose from an ordinary gardeners boy! Everyone was astounded and delighted. ... I was more impressed by the scene I had witnessed than words can say, proud of all that had passed and of my beloved's success. Dearest Albert's name is for ever immortalized, and the absurd reports of dangers of every kind and sort, put out by a set of people—the *soi disant* 'fashionables' and the violent protectionists—are silenced. ...

With the opening ceremony safely over the Exhibition began its 141 days of triumphant life during which the building, the Crystal Palace itself, was of far greater attraction than anything it contained. Unlike the second Great International Exhibition in 1862, held in a building nicknamed the Brompton Boilers which was described as 'hideous outside and overcrowded within,' the Crystal Palace came in for unreserved praise, although many critics expressed many reservations about many of the exhibits.

Several 'dam' great thick' books could be written about the contents of the Crystal Palace and the light they shine upon the industrial, artistic and social life of the time. On opening day many of the foreign exhibits were still in disarray in the side aisles, and because the Baltic ports were late in thawing, the Russian contributions were not in place until the end of May; but as the Palace contained far more than could be digested in one visit, or even a dozen, these lacunae scarcely mattered.

The exhibits can only briefly be summarized here. There were thirty sub-divisions to the five main classes which were: *Raw Materials*, which ranged from the dull to the bizarre, from the biggest lump of coal ever mined in one piece to a bundle of peacock feathers; *Machinery*, more particularly *Machinery in Motion* which was impressive, ingenious and not infrequently beautiful; *Manufactures*, *Textile Fabrics*, which would probably most appeal to late twentieth-century taste despite such inevitable absurdities as a 'pair of cuffs hand-spun and knitted from the wool of French poodle dogs'; *Manufactures, Metallic Vitreous and Ceramic,* which included much fine and some deplorable china and glass, beautiful watches, technically excellent clocks mostly in hideous cases, admirable iron and steel work of all kinds just tottering on the edge of over-elaboration and a great many gold, silver and electro-plated objects which had fallen over it into an abyss of unparalleled vulgarity and bad design; *Miscellaneous,* which included most of the absurdities, and the domestic furniture and appliances nearly all of which displayed in high degree the Victorian failings of coy, mawkish sentimentality coupled with the belief that the more difficult a thing was to do, the more obdurate the material and the more elaborately inconsequential the super-abundance of incongruous applied ornamentation, the better the thing must be. There were so many examples in which obduracy of material was combined with the 'every-picture-tells-a-story' form of art that one specimen may serve to illustrate all. This was an arm chair of debased Louis XVI style, standing on heavily carved cabriole legs suffering from a severe attack of elephantiasis, with its exposed framing of deeply carved Irish bog-oak, a material which resists the carver's efforts even more stoutly than *lignum vitae.* The arms of this monstrosity were tortured into the likenesses of Irish wolf-hounds with mottoes carved on their collars: one was erect, snarling and labelled 'Fierce when Provoked', whilst the other was recumbent, sleeping and proclaimed itself to be 'Gentle when Stroked'.

Lastly came *Fine Arts,* sub-divided into *Sculpture, Models (in Architecture, Topography and Anatomy)* and *Plastic Art.* All other art forms were excluded and the Commissioners also wisely excluded works more than three years old. Therefore the Fine Arts display was largely of modern sculpture which, like so much of the furniture, combined technical excellence with cloying sentimentality. T. and M. Thornycroft exhibited a very fine equestrian statue of the Queen on her horse Hammon, whilst T. and A. Thornycroft showed a figure of the young Prince of Wales as an idealized Greek shepherd which might well have been conceived by Disney and manufactured by the Plastic Gnome Corporation. The naked female form was perfectly acceptable to the Victorians provided it was designed to 'point the moral and adorn the tale'. Hence the overwhelming popularity of Hiram Power's Greek Slave which the exhibitor's panegyric described as:

The figure here represented is intended for that of a young and beautiful Greek girl, deprived of her clothing and exposed for sale to some wealthy eastern barbarian, before whom she is supposed to stand, with an expression of scornful dejection mingled with shame and disgust. Her dress, which is the modern Greek costume, appears on the column, and the cross implies her religion and country. The chains on her wrists are not historical, but have been added as necessary accessories.

The slender chains slung from wrist to wrist could, indeed, serve no purpose but to draw attention to the lady's pudendum, across which they were draped in supposed modesty.

There were also a number of statues cast in zinc, which was then a relatively new material for casting, and in these the sculptors' determination to show their mastery of a new technique outweighed their artistic abilities. Before we scoff, however, let us remember that one of the most admired exhibits at the 1924 British Empire Exhibition at Wembley was a life-size but far from life-like statue of the Prince of Wales, which was intended simultaneously to advertise New Zealand's principal export and to proclaim her loyalty by being executed in butter.

Many of the exhibits appeared to have been designed by the White Knight to demonstrate that misplaced ingenuity can always triumph over common sense. Thus, Count Dunin's life-size metal figure of a man, which could be expanded to nearly twice life-size by turning a handle and goading into action more than five thousand concealed moving parts, was awarded a Council Medal, although this brilliantly conceived miracle of needless complexity was self-evidently useless. An exhibit which went almost unnoticed came from Hanover. Thanks to the old King's opposition (he died a month after the Exhibition closed), the protectionist Northern States, which came within the aegis of Hanover's *Steuerverein* which Ernest Augustus had set up in opposition to Prussia's *Zollverein*, were very meagrely represented. Hanover herself sent only ten items but one of these was the Morse electric telegraph. This admirable instrument, with its now universal, simple, code of long or short sounds, went unnoticed, whilst the Press and the public went into raptures over Smith's Comic Electric Telegraph. This instrument, if such it can be called, resembled the face of a ventriloquist's dummy and was supposed to deliver its messages by various combinations of its galvanically twitching lips, eyebrows and rolling eyeballs.

Resisting the temptation to linger over such tantalizing (and presumably anti-gravitational) delights as the pair of 'Anaxyridian Trousers' which, the *Catalogue* proclaimed, were so shaped 'that they remain as a fixture to the heel without straps, and dispense with braces', the rest of the exhibits must be reduced to numbers. There were, as stated earlier, 13,937 exhibitors showing approximately 112,000 individual items. Excluding some of the raw materials and farm machinery which were shown outside, these occupied 338,714 square feet of horizontal space and 653,143 square feet vertically; yet with all this space filled with goods, and with nearly 100,000 people in the building at one time, the Crystal Palace never seemed overcrowded.

The success of the Exhibition is best judged by the numbers who visited it. The total of 6,039,195 is impressive by any standard and could not have been achieved in the pre-railway age when stage coach fares of 6d. a mile had to be set against day-labourers' wages of 10½d. The railways also, of course, made a contribution to the speed with which the building was erected, and contemporary observers had been impressed by the fact that it was possible to erect columns and girders eighteen hours after they had been in the molten state in Fox and Henderson's foundry.

The other reason for the very large attendance was the Commission's sensible policy about admission charges. After 31 July the season tickets were reduced from three and two guineas to 30s. and £1.00. On the two days following the opening, £1.00 was charged; then from 5 to 24 May the price was 5s.; on and after 26 May, from Monday to Thursday, the charge was only 1s. with Fridays at 2s. 6d. and Saturdays at 5s. From 9 August Saturday admission was also reduced to 2s. 6d.

The Exhibition was closed on Sundays and was therefore open for 141 days; the attendance figures break down as follows:

Season Ticket holders	141 days		773,766
£1.00 visitors	2	,,	1,042
5/- visitors ·	28	,,	245,389
2/6 visitors	30	,,	579,579
1/- visitors	80	,,	4,439,419
			6,039,195

The average daily attendance was 42,831 and the greatest number admitted on one day (7 October 1851) was 109,915. The greatest number in the building at one time on that day was 93,224.

On that day also, 7 October, the only serious mishap occurred during the life of the Exhibition. 'Serious' is perhaps an overstatement as the trouble occasioned no more than some broken china and the ruffling of the Duke of Wellington's temper. When the crowd was at its height the Duke appeared on the scene. He was almost as frequent a visitor as the Queen and, like her, he often arrived before opening time and left as soon as crowds began to flock in, but invariably he was noticed and cheered. When he arrived after opening time he tried to escape notice by using the private door to the Commissioners' office or the Royal entrance, as though these subterfuges would envelop him in a cloak of invisibility for the rest of the day. Henry Cole wrote of what happened on 7 October.

> 109,000 visitors were in the building this day. When at its fullest, 93,000 present, the Duke of Wellington came, and although cautioned by the police, he would walk up the nave in the midst of the crowd. He was soon recognized and cheered. The distant crowds were alarmed, and someone raised the cry that 'the building was falling'. There was a rush. Fortunately six policemen had followed the Duke, and literally carried him off, pale and indignant, by the side passages, as I saw when coming out of my office. The crowds upset a stand of French Pallisy ware, and the first persons to get out of the building were the sentries. Nothing worse happened, and it was the only accident during the Exhibition.

In addition to the Exhibition being closed on Sundays, smoking was prohibited and the sale of alcohol forbidden. This was probably a wise precaution, but it strikes the only depressing note in the history of the Exhibition to read that 1,092,337 bottles of soft drinks were sold, together with 943,691 Bath buns and 870,027 plain ones as well as 'a variety of other eatables'. Not only were the eatables and drinkables uninspiring by nature, they were poor in quality, outrageously expensive and served by waitresses who were described as dirty and inattentive. The badness of railway refreshment room provender was already firmly established as a joke in the poorest of taste (almost literally), and the Crystal Palace restaurants appear barely to have reached railway buffet standards. The restaurant contracts were let to a famous soft drinks company, who may be presumed to have laid the foundations of their present prosperity on the Crystal Palace as they charged sixpence of good Victorian money for 'little dry dollops of pork pie', as one complainant wrote, less than half the size of those sold for a penny in many public houses. Other prices were comparable. Letter writers to *The Times* or the *Morning Chronicle*, including, no doubt, our old friends 'Pro Bono Publico', 'Paterfamilias' and 'Disgusted' of Tunbridge Wells, dipped their pens in vitriol on the subject and a typical example, from the *Morning Chronicle*, reads:

> Pray assist to remedy a most universal complaint of all those hungry curious at the Great Exhibition, by giving the young females at the refreshment tables a hint that their personal appearances, as well as their hands and faces, would be greatly improved by a moderate use of soap. The excuse of not having had time since the 1st. of May to wash themselves certainly appears true, but the contractor would do well, in case of increasing business, to have relays of washed damsels if he wishes to see his eatables well digested.

This letter upholds the heartless Victorian tradition of seeing the working class as 'the lower orders' and 'the great unwashed', but the Exhibition played a part in bridging the gulf between the two nations. The Crystal Palace was a place in which 'the pounds and the shillings', as *Punch* put it, could meet, and to their reiterated amazement the pounds saw that the shillings were not the filthy, foul-mouthed, drunken brutes they feared, but shabby, clean, orderly men quietly enjoying a rare treat with their wives and children. Even at a shilling the expense was too great for the really poor, but thanks to excursion rates on the railways and to the organization by working men's associations, parish parsons and others, parties of industrial and agricultural labourers, with their families, were able to come from all parts of the country at an average price of half a crown apiece, including admission. Obviously, not all of the four and a half million shilling tickets were sold to working-class customers, but a large proportion were and the Crystal Palace really was the first place in which Duke and Dustman could meet on equal terms. Everybody but Colonel Sibthorp appears to have been delighted that this was so, and he chose a new ground for attack in the House of Commons where he trumpeted on 29 July, 1851 :

> Unfortunately, however, for the people of this country, the erection of this Crystal Palace took place; and what has been the result? The desecration of the Sabbath—the demoralization of the people—a disunion of parties —and increasing poverty to a most serious extent; for I have heard, and with pain, that the poor of this country have been seduced to come up to this Exhibition. All that they had saved and all they could borrow has been in many cases spent on this foolish journey; and I know I speak facts when I state that not only have they borrowed money but pawned their clothes to enable them to come up to this 'World's Fair', as it was called; and now they are left without a penny in their pockets....

That the Great Exhibition did nothing to promote long-term peace and brotherhood between nations is certain, and certainly not surprising. With a few honourable exceptions nothing it contained served to elevate taste and improve the artistic standards of manufactured objects; indeed, it may even have accelerated the decline which had set in after the Regency. On the more serious side of the business, industrialists from different countries may have had a few salutary shocks as they examined what their rivals were doing, and a fairly casual eye could have detected, for example, that the trade in watches specially designed for the Chinese market had passed from England and France to the horological parvenu, Switzerland. A handful of British farmers may have taken up McCormick's reaping machine from America a few years earlier than they would otherwise have done; sales of London-made carriages in Paris and Vienna may have been augmented and so forth. The irrefutable if intangible benefit from the Great Exhibition, however, was that more than six million people were given pleasure by it; and the chief source of that pleasure was the Crystal Palace itself.

In all the thousands of words written by those who visited the Exhibition, from the Queen downwards, it is impossible to find one which damns the building. It is no exaggeration to say that no building has been better fitted for its purpose than the Crystal Palace, in addition to which its beauty gave pleasure to all who saw it. Even Sibthorp conceded, 'It is, no doubt, a wonderful building externally' (he refused to enter it), and many visitors echoed the Queen's verdict, 'The building is so light and graceful, in spite of its immense size.'

By the end of July, when it must sometimes have seemed that no topic of private or public interest other than the Exhibition existed, and when all London's regular tourist attractions were booming as a result of it, the question of what was to happen to the Crystal Palace began to be aired. The country in general and Londoners in particular had taken the place so much to heart that there were many in favour of keeping the Exhibition open through the winter. The Commissioners were adamant that it must close, as planned, on 15 October; if for no other reason than that there was insufficient gas-light installed, which became obvious towards the middle of September when visitors had to be 'rung out' at sunset rather than at 6 o'clock. What of the building itself? Almost as loud an outcry against dismantling it was raised as had been heard against the original proposal to build in Hyde Park. Paxton had the idea of turning it into a Winter Garden, and rather imprudently repeated his tactic of ventilating this notion through the *Illustrated London News*. He gained a good deal of support, but not from the Commissioners or the Government. Nor was the Prince in favour as the Queen recorded in her *Journal*:

> Lord John [Lord John Russell, Prime Minister] came at 4. Talked ... of the address of the Hse of C. relative to the Crystal Palace. Ld John seemed very fair and reason-

he Opening Ceremony. The official painting by Henry C. Selous, with the bogus
hinese mandarin well to the fore

for this vote could be made to the Crown.

It was a question whether this exhibition should be
exclusively limited to British Industry. It was considered that,
whilst it appears an error to fix any limitation
advantages would arise from collecting the scattered productions
to the productions of Machinery, Science & Taste
of all nations and that foreign productions ought not to
which any of our country [?] belong as a whole.
be excluded the occasion should be one in which the visits
to the Civilized world, particular advantage
of Foreigners to England should be encouraged [?]
to British Industry might be derived from
[?] placing it in fair competition with that of other
It was required that such Industrial Machinery and Nations.—

enry Cole's Memorandum. This contains the first suggestion that the Exhibition
iould be international in scope, altered and made more emphatic by Prince Albert

An Outdoor Display. Agricultural implements, including a 'portable' steam engine of the type used to drive the wood-working and metal-punching machines

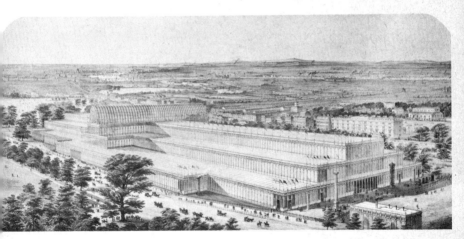

The Exterior at Hyde Park. One of the less fanciful of the contemporary engravings, this artist's viewpoint is of the north-west corner, but he has had to 'remove' several trees

The Interior. Taken before people were about, this is a Fox Talbot calotype which shows the cast-iron Coalbrookdale gates and the crystal fountain

The East End of the Building. A contemporary calotype in which the blurring of the flags indicates the length of the exposure needed

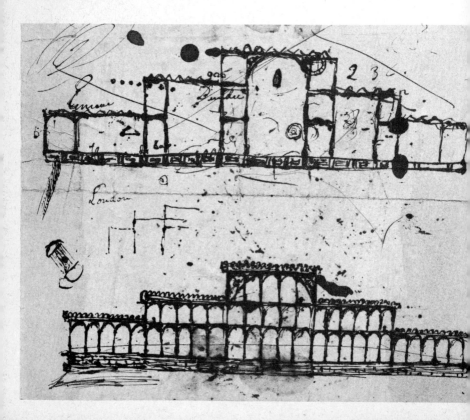

denham: Building the South Water Tower. This wrought-iron skeleton eventually
grew to be a ferro-concrete giant, 284 ft. high and capable of holding 300,000
gallons

xton's Design on a blotting-paper rough

Aeronautical View of the Sydenham Crystal Palace. From a painting by C. J. Ashford based on a photograph taken in 1919, this shows the asymmetrical shape of the building after the north transept was destroyed by fire in 1866

efore the Fire of 1866. The north transept with its Egyptian statuary

Messrs Brock's Firework
Displays. A well-remembered
feature of the Sydenham
Palace, these show a pyro-
technic portrait of the Duke
of Wellington and the Battle
of Manila Bay

Real Fireworks. The 1936 disaster

able about the latter, and we discussed the pros and
cons. There were many who wished the Palace to
remain for the honour of the Country and the Exhibition—others, precisely for the same reason, feared that
the building might fall into decay and therefore wished
it to come down—others, again, wished it to be turned
into a Winter Garden. Others, and in this Ld Seymour
is very much to the fore, think that the Govt should
not break faith with the public, and for that reason it
ought to come down and a new one be built. Albert is
likewise in favor of this, and we discussed all the points
and different plans as to what should be done with the
large surplus. . . .

The Queen's reference to the wish for a 'new one' to be
built is puzzling, as the proposal to rebuild the Palace on
another site did not materialize until later. So, with the
future of the building undecided the finality of the mid-
October closing was underlined. The 15th fell on a Wednesday and on the Monday and Tuesday only guests of the
Exhibitors and Commissioners were admitted. The Queen
came early on each day, and wrote of her last visit: 'Each
time one is amazed afresh at the immense length and height,
and the fairy-like effect. . . . Walked in fact through the
whole building bidding it regretfully adieu. . . .'
The closing ceremony itself was watched by a crowd
estimated at 40-50,000 people, though one is tempted to
think it cannot have been a very inspiring sight as those
in the galleries can have seen little but the balding heads of
the Commissioners seated round a large table on a dais at
the intersection of nave and transept, whilst those at ground
level would have had little on which to fix their gaze but a
row of broadcloth-covered posteriors perched on a motley
collection of chairs perilously near the edge of the platform.
As the occasion was really no more than a glorified meeting
of the Commissioners the Queen was not present, to her
regret, as she could not take second place to her husband
who presided. He was enthroned at the head of the table

117

on the most uncomfortable chair in the building, a monstrous, high, ornately carved ivory affair, complete with two-tier footstool-cum-approach-ladder, presented to the Queen (who sadly typified the taste of her age by describing it as 'beautiful') by the Rajah of Travancore.

The business, which must have been totally inaudible to the spectators, began with the National Anthem, followed by a very long report read by Lord Canning on behalf of the various juries who had judged the exhibits (their decisions and awards, perhaps, inevitably, satisfied few and offended many); the Prince read a long reply, God Save the Queen was sung again, the Bishop of London prayed and the Great Exhibition closed as it had opened with the Hallelujah Chorus.

With the Exhibition closed came the time to cast accounts. Fox and Henderson's extra expenses were finally settled at £35,000, and Paxton was given a well-deserved honorarium of £5,000. Reckoning in these sums the total cost of the building, taken on its permanent structure basis, was £190,000. The full sum of expenses was £335,742; receipts £522,179 and the profit, therefore, £186,437. Paxton, Fox and Cubitt were knighted. Dilke's conscience would not allow him to accept public honours so the Queen gave his wife a ruby bracelet and, as is the common lot of those who work in the background, Henry Cole* was fobbed off with the C.B. and a letter of thanks from the Prince.

Within a fortnight the Great Exhibition was succeeded by Kossuth's arrival in England as a focus for public attention, and Louis Napoleon's elevation of himself into an Emperor completed the eclipse a few weeks later.

There were two questions still unanswered. What was to be done with the profit? and what was to happen to the Crystal Palace?

* He was knighted in 1875 for his work in creating the South Kensington Museum (now the Victoria and Albert), and for his public service in many other fields, notably the Government Schools of Design.

9 To Sydenham

Once when speaking at the Mechanics' Institute in Derby Joseph Paxton was reported as saying he 'believed it was a good thing to have the conceit taken out of us.' Whilst he did not undervalue himself Paxton was the least conceited of men although enough adulation was heaped upon him for his Crystal Palace to turn anybody's head. Some of the praise, such as that which compared him not unfavourably with Sir Christopher Wren, was ludicrously overdone; but *Punch* caught the public enthusiasm for the Palace and the disgust with the expensive and long-delayed new Houses of Parliament by appealing to Paxton to house Lords and Commons quickly, cheaply and commodiously in two of his splendid Glass Houses:

> It is now clear Mr Barry will never finish his structure. Two millions of money are already doomed upon an uncertain, unsatisfactory pile. Sir, you can do it in a morning. You have only to don your working coat, to clap on your considering cap—that pretty tasteful thing bent from a leaf of the *Victoria regia*—and the matter is done. Say the word Mr Paxton; shall the Queen next February open the new Houses of Glass? All we want is your promise. For us the princely Devonshire bears honourable and honouring testimony that Mr Paxton

has never attempted anything which he has not succeeded in fully carrying out. ...' Mr Paxton you *must*
achieve the Glass Houses of Parliament. Here and there
you can insert a pane of magnifying power to make
any favourite Minister look a greater man than he
is.

This did nothing beyond making Barry resent Paxton's
success, and the Houses of Parliament were to drag on for
another ten years; and when at last they were done, in 1860,
structural and other faults were already manifest in some
parts of a building which had been started in 1840.

In Exhibition year almost everybody who could wield
a pen wielded it in praise of Mr Paxton and a necessary,
though rather chilling, corrective came from Ruskin who
protested against the 'delusion that we had invented a new
style of architecture when we had magnified a conservatory.'
Here, perhaps, Ruskin was a little unkind as ferro-vitreous
(or ferro-concrete-vitreous) buildings are now commonplace, but in *The Stones of Venice* he summarized his
opinion:

The value of every work of art is exactly in the ratio
of the quantity of humanity which has been put into
it, and elgibly expressed upon it for ever: First, of
thought and moral purpose. Secondly, of technical skill.
Thirdly, of bodily industry.

The quantity of bodily industry which that Crystal
Palace expresses is very great. So far it is good. The
quantity of thought it expresses is, I suppose, a single
and very admirable thought of Sir Joseph Paxton's—
probably not a bit brighter than thousands of thoughts
which pass through his active and intelligent brain
every hour—that it might be possible to build a greenhouse larger than ever greenhouse was built before.
This thought, and some very ordinary algebra, are as
much as all that glass can represent of human intellect.

The passage betrays Ruskin's contempt for the technical skill
to which he paid lip-service, and is bedevilled by the attempt
to judge a building—or a picture or piece of furniture—in
terms of moral purpose. Most of Paxton's contemporaries
probably felt more in sympathy with the opening stanza of
Thackeray's *May-Day Ode*:

> But yesterday a naked sod
> The dandies sneered from Rotten Row,
> And cantered o'er it to and fro:
> And see 'tis done!
> As though 'twere by a wizard's rod
> A blazing arch of lucid glass
> Leaps like a fountain from the grass
> To meet the sun!

Though he remained unconceited Joseph Paxton, Sir
Joseph now and soon to be Member of Parliament for
Coventry, did not hesitate to pull all the strings available
to him to keep the Crystal Palace in Hyde Park. His idea of
making it a 'Winter Garden', or permanent 'leisure centre'
as modern jargon would depressingly call it, had been formed
as early as September 1850, and his pamphlet *What is to
become of the Crystal Palace?* was widely read and as widely
supported by such papers as *The Times*, the *Morning Post*,
Punch and the *Illustrated London News*. He presented a
petition to Parliament in July 1851 praying for the retention
of the Palace on its site, other petitions flowed in and Lord
Shaftesbury lent his considerable influence to the Winter
Garden project by presiding over a large public meeting in
the Exeter Hall where such generally opposed voices as those
of Joseph Hume and the Duke of Argyll also spoke in
support.

Successful men never want for enemies, however, and just
as, after his death, a baseless rumour was set afoot by the
Derbyshire Courier that Paxton had 'stolen' the design for
the Crystal Palace from one of the Chatsworth estate
workers named Marples, so there were a few critics ready

to accuse him of self-aggrandizement and money-grubbing over the Winter Garden project. There was merit in the plan because the London of the 1850s had few places of respectable entertainment, none that a woman of good reputation could enter unaccompanied, no restaurants between the few expensive hotels, the city chop-houses (exclusively male) and working-class 'dining rooms' which were often fronts for brothels, and no place under cover in which to stage large-scale concert or orchestral performances.

Of the money-grubbing accusation one cannot do better than quote Paxton's biographer, Violet Markham, who wrote :

> Paxton was convinced that the retention of the Palace in its original site was a matter of public importance. That conviction was inspired by more laudable aims than the natural wish of an architect to rescue his work from oblivion. Chatsworth, and all that life at Chatsworth implied, had never dimmed Paxton's sympathies for the hard lot of the struggling masses. His work did not lie in the field of philanthropy or social reform, but over a long term of years his written and spoken word reveal a warm-hearted desire to promote better education, better conditions, better opportunities for the working classes. An article ... published in 1833 in his *Horticultural Register* on the condition of the British peasantry, was startling at that date in its frank statement of the callousness of the rich and the miseries of the poor. Paxton never lost his hold on these realities. ... He knew the struggles and limitations of the class from which he had sprung. In later life, as a wealthy man, he did not smite his breast and exploit his humble birth on public platforms. But he never forgot those early days; wholly devoid as he was of snobbery, he felt no false shame about them. In the Crystal Palace he saw an instrument that would, in his opinion, make a great contribution to the education and the happiness of the masses. That instrument, he felt, at all costs must be

preserved. ... He fought, and he fought hard, for the life of his child.

As the Queen's journal and one of his own memoranda make clear Prince Albert was one of those who opposed Paxton's Winter Garden scheme. Very properly, he made no public comment but was privately unmoved by the many letters the Commissioners received or which *The Times*, and other papers, published urging that the Crystal Palace should stay. Lord Carlisle wrote to say that its destruction would be 'a perverse and senseless act of vandalism', whilst others preferred a more easterly location for wanton acts and called the proposed removal 'Byzantine'.

The Government made no useful contribution to the question of what should be done with the profits of the Exhibition, and on the fate of the building they took their stand on the narrow plank of the pledge to remove it. In view of the public clamour to keep it where it was there would have been fairly general approval if they had asked Parliament to release the Commissioners from their undertaking. The view Prince Albert expressed in his memorandum, that the Commissioners had no power to divert any part of the profit towards supplying Londoners with a place of entertainment, could have been over-ruled, but although the Government's refusal to look further than the legalistic aspect seemed narrow-minded at the time history has proved it to be right, even if only fortuitously. It can be seen now that as the novelty wore off, as London grew, as social habits changed and as other places of entertainment sprang up pressure would ultimately have developed to remove the Palace on the grounds that it had become an unprofitable, shabby, old-fashioned bore. If it had to go it were better that it went at once in a blaze of glory.

All through the winter of 1851 and into the spring of 1852 the empty Palace still attracted thousands who came to stare at its glittering bulk and graceful colonnades. A few exhibits which were too large to be easily moved or too silly to be endurable still stood about, and occasional band per-

formances were held in the transept. Parliament did not
resolve the question until 30 April 1852 when the decision
to order the removal of the Crystal Palace was carried by a
majority of 118. Colonel Sibthorp surpassed himself with a
final tirade of pompous invective. He begged that Parliament
would at last come to its senses for long enough to command
the removal of a transparent humbug, a palace of tomfoolery,
stuffed with foreign rubbish, in which the poor had been
trepanned, ensnared, humbugged and seduced out of their
hard-won earnings. This sight of the place made him sick—
and objects had been photographed on the Sabbath. . . .

Parliament's decision might have been expected to depress
Joseph Paxton, but the Duke of Devonshire's *Diary* for the
following day recorded: 'Crystal Palace condemned yester-
day by the House of Commons, so it comes down. Paxton
was here this morning in good spirits.' Paxton was too
shrewd a man to put all his eggs into one basket, and he had
already prepared a contingency plan. This was to set up a
private company to buy the Crystal Palace and to re-erect
it on some other suitable site so that the Winter Garden
project could go ahead untrammelled by Governments or
Royal Commissions.

Just as he had done when he first submitted his building
plan Paxton had taken preliminary soundings, and as early
as 7 April he had written to his wife to say he could count
on raising half a million of capital without difficulty should
it become necessary. By 18 May the Crystal Palace Company
Limited had been duly floated with the projected £500,000
capital in £5 shares. Very soon thereafter contracts were
exchanged for the purchase of a superb site on the top and
eastern slopes of Sydenham Hill; the Crystal Palace was
bought from the Commissioners for £75,000, and Fox and
Henderson were contracted to dismantle, transport and re-
erect it for a further £120,000.

To say that the history of the first period of the Crystal
Palace—from the blotting-paper sketch to the much-lamented
closing—was unruffled would be ludicrous; but the business
had gone with remarkably few setbacks and those few

remarkably easily overcome. The history of the second period is studded with delays, setbacks and disappointments leading to a long period of shabby-genteel decay and a tragic end. This has led many writers to dismiss the long second life as one of unmitigated failure and the rebuilt Palace as a colossal white elephant. This is unfair: although the Crystal Palace Company never made a profit and ended in bankruptcy, the Palace itself enjoyed twenty to thirty years of popularity after its transfer to Sydenham, and was emerging from the doldrums again when the end came.

The basis of the trouble was that the half-million of capital was not enough and so the project was financially crippled from the start. There is an element of truth in the obvious suggestion that Paxton had ideas above his station and planned on far too grandiose a scale. As we have seen, he was a shrewd businessman whose scheme for dealing with what he and his wife called The Great Debt on the Devonshire estates had been accepted by the Duke's conventional advisers and had been largely successful. Nevertheless, Paxton was himself responsible for creating the Great Debt to the extent that his passion for improving and beautifying the estates encouraged the Duke's natural tendency towards extravagance. Both were modest in their personal tastes but wholly unable to resist spending on the grand scale to achieve a grand object. It would be wrong to say Paxton went ahead regardless of expense, but the expense had to be extraordinarily outrageous to cause him to stay his hand. As early as 1838, for example, with an amazing leap towards the future, Paxton bewailed that the electric light was too expensive to use as a sort of artificial sun to help the propagation and growth of some of the rarer and more delicate plants he grew for the Duke. As the few electric arc-lights set up in Vauxhall Gardens in celebration of Queen Victoria's coronation in that year required serried ranks of primary batteries which consumed four thousand pounds' worth of zinc and acids in a single night one does see why Paxton drew back; but on the other hand he did not flinch from installing a primitive form of outdoor soil heating, using concealed furnace flues running through artificial banks to coax some of the more tender exotics to thrive in a hostile climate. Even in those days of cheap coal this was a fairly bizarre extravagance.

The new site for the Crystal Palace was so splendid that it cried out to Paxton for landscaping on the most lavish scale. The suburban development of Sydenham, Penge and Anerley only materialized after the Palace was moved there, and the few houses on the western and northern slopes were largish 'villas' each enjoying the seclusion of three or four well-wooded acres. To the east and south the ground sloped steeply away and commanded unspoilt views over part of Surrey and on to the Kentish hills in the distance. The villages of Bromley, Sidcup, Wickham and others were no more than remote rustic hamlets almost invisible in the wooded landscape beneath.

Although he had overall direction of many matters, including the rebuilding and furnishing of the Palace itself, the Company's prospectus described Paxton by the modest title of Director of Gardens which were, indeed, his sole creation. Fashions in gardens and parks have changed so many times since the 1850s that it is now difficult to say by how much the Crystal Palace grounds merited the praise lavished upon them as they grew to maturity, or the scathing denunciation heaped upon them in the early part of this century.

Just as the railway had made possible the swift, cheap transportation of the iron and glass for the Crystal Palace from Birmingham to London (the timber came by road from the London docks), so the different railway companies, notably the Great Northern, had benefited greatly from the passenger traffic generated by the Exhibition. From its inception the new Crystal Palace Company was closely bound to the railway system; the Company's Chairman, Samuel Laing, was also Chairman of the London, Brighton and South Coast Railway Company which was itself a majority shareholder in the Crystal Palace concern. The L.B. & S.C. laid an additional down line from their London

Bridge terminus with a branch coming in to the Palace grounds near their lowest point. This was later known as the Low Level Station and return tickets for eighteen pence from London Bridge covered the cut-price fivepenny fare and 1/1 admission money to the Crystal Palace. Another branch line, rather grandly known as the West End of London and Crystal Palace Railway Company, was worked by the L.B. & S.C. company and ran from the wilds of Wandsworth Common, as it then was, to the Palace. This was ultimately linked to Victoria when the London to Brighton line was carried across the river to this new terminus. In the early 1860s the London, Chatham and Dover Railway Company (irreverently known to the Victorians as the London, Smashem and Turnover) also laid a line and established the High Level Station adjoining the Palace near the top of the hill; this line was extended over the Thames to Ludgate Hill and Farringdon Street in 1864, and this branch in its turn was connected by the Metropolitan Railway to King's Cross so there was direct rail access from the North and Midlands to the Crystal Palace.

Unfortunately the first rail link, to the Low Level Station, was not finished until after the reopening and the Crystal Palace Company's initial takings suffered accordingly. Also, the absence of a railway made the removal of the Palace from Hyde Park rather more difficult and almost as costly as the original transportation of the raw materials from the Midlands. The original journey had involved short and level horse-and-cart journeys at either end of the railway, and bringing the timber from the London docks had actually cost more than carrying the iron and glass from Birmingham.

The work of dismantling the Palace went ahead very quickly. Understandably, a large proportion of the glass was broken, but the contractors had allowed for this and Chance Brothers remelted and remade the panes at small cost. Dismantling the bolted framework was even easier than putting it together, but moving the pieces to their new home was far from easy. The distance was little more than twelve miles as the crow flies, but crow-transport would not do and the road journey involved more than twenty fairly formidable miles for horse-drawn wagons through crowded streets to the nearest bridge across the Thames (the Chelsea, Battersea and Albert bridges did not then exist), then over a succession of hills to the horse-killing obstacle of Sydenham Hill itself. When it is considered that the gentle slope of Kensington Church Street was considered severe enough to warrant hitching on a 'cock horse' to the ordinary pair-horse omnibuses, the long, winding slope of Sydenham Hill with its one-in-eight gradient can be judged with the eye of a mid-Victorian carter with two exhausted beasts in front and a couple of tons of ironwork behind. One of the first fruits of the Crystal Palace's removal was the formation of an Animal Protection Society, supported by voluntary contributions, to provide trace horses at subsidized prices, a penny against the sixpence charged commercially, to help haul heavy loads up Sydenham Hill. This body was not only one of the first of its kind but the first to use machinery to help animals, and by 1900 the Society's trace horses had been transmogrified into a pair of Tasker's 'Little Giant' traction engines.

When the materials did reach the summit Fox and Henderson faced a much more daunting task than in Hyde Park. The site sloped towards the east and it was thought better to add a basement on that side of the Palace rather than to level the ground. This was well enough but Paxton and his fellow Directors decided to enlarge and improve the building in order to make it a fitting crown to such a splendid vantage point. Because the addition of the part-basement altered the proportions of the building as seen from the grounds to the east it was necessary to lengthen the already long building, and because the barrel-vaulted transept had been so much admired in Hyde Park it was decided to add a semi-circular roof along the entire length of the nave; in order that the central transept should still stand above the rest of the building it then became necessary to raise it by two more tiers, but in order to keep its proportions in relationship with the rest of the enlarged building it was also necessary to make it almost twice its original width; in order that so large a central transept should not dominate the building too completely it was then thought necessary to add two more, smaller, barrel-vaulted transepts, one to each half of the nave four-fifths of the distance from the centre. Therefore the three-tier building with a central transept became six storeys high in part, with three transepts, containing nearly twice the amount of glass as the original and with all other materials increased in proportion. This great increase in the size and cost of the building may not have made sense financially but proved the flexibility of the original plan.

Paxton's plans for the grounds included lavish water displays, fountains, cascades, falls, fast-running brooks and artificial lakes. He hoped to rival Versailles and to outdo Chatsworth, but at Chatsworth he was able, as his predecessors had done, to harness the abundant streams on the hills high above the park. At Sydenham every drop had to be pumped, and as the various water displays demanded 120,000 gallons a minute when all were in full play they far out-reached the capacity of the local pumping station and steam-driven pumps to fill supplementary reservoirs had to be installed to augment the supply. The reservoirs were in the form of twin water towers, with the pumping machinery in the bases and the flues rising through the tanks which each held 300,000 gallons. The towers stood 284 ft. high and because the water alone in each weighed 3,000 tons Isambard Brunel, who designed them, guarded against slip on the sloping, clay-bottomed site by providing exceptionally deep foundations of Portland cement surmounted by brickwork cones rising to ground level. The towers themselves were of a new material, ferro-concrete with stiffening diaphragms of wrought iron in each of their ten storeys. They proved difficult to build and the estimated price was exceeded almost twofold, just as Fox and Henderson's estimate was exceeded nearly four times by the time the greatly altered and enlarged Palace was completed. The enormous cost of keeping the water displays functioning proved too much for the Company, and by 1930 the twelve thousand jets, the cascades and other watery delights had long been dry in silted-up pools or basins.

The actual construction of the 'new' Crystal Palace followed the Hyde Park pattern and needs no comment. Possibly to save cost some of the new material did not match the old. For example, in the new transepts the columns were plainly cylindrical instead of the part-curved, part-flat octagons which had lent themselves so readily to Owen Jones's scheme of parti-coloured decoration. Having simplified the columns in this way the contractors must then have spent any money they saved by fixing needless, ornamental, fussy, spandrel brackets below each junction of column and girder. The first column at Sydenham was raised on 5 August 1852, but because of the various difficulties and alterations the building was still to be completed when the Queen opened it on 10 June 1854. Worse than the difficulties and the extra expense was a terrible accident which killed twelve men. The greatly shocked Paxton felt personally responsible for this and though the Duke of Devonshire still had first call on his services, he bought a large house, Rockhills, a few minutes' walk from the Palace and supervised nearly all that went on until his death in 1865.

The interior fitments, such as floors and gas lamps, were much more elaborate and expensive than in the original building, and because the interior was much less open the effect of airy spaciousness so apparent in Hyde Park was lessened.

The purpose of the rebuilt Crystal Palace was to combine recreation with education in a manner which the late twentieth century might consider daunting. A vast concert hall with room for an audience of 4,000, and almost as many performers, dominated by a huge organ (finished in 1857) occupied the central space at the intersection of nave and main transept. The concerts, and in particular the Handel festivals, held here on a scale previously impossible in England became world famous, and during the opening ceremony Clara Novello, singing the solo parts of the

National Anthem, reached a high B-flat of such electrifying power that all the policemen present raised their helmets in the air contrary to precedent and discipline. More importantly, Madam Novello's triumphant trumpeting was held to have proven the safety of the building for all time.

Restaurants occupied parts of the east face of the building and commanded splendid views of the gardens, fountains and, after 1865, Messrs Brock's fireworks displays for which the Crystal Palace was famed. Dining at the Crystal Palace became the 'done thing' of the 1860s and 70s. Nor was the treat confined to the middle class, *The Graphic* recording in 1870:

> You may enjoy an unrivalled prospect from the Grand Saloon Dining Room in the Crystal Palace. Fountains spout silvery streams, and indigo tints from summer nights are lit up by the firework festival's glories. The price of dinner is from five shillings to four guineas. A second-class dinner for humbler customers is twenty pence, a third-class one, beer included, being half that amount.

To complement the rare plants and trees outside the building Paxton used part of his great glass house *as* a glasshouse, with part of the nave devoted to displays of tropical palms and other plants mostly from the famous Loddige collection. To the great annoyance of Napoleon III (who could equally well have bought them) Paxton also brought King Louis-Philippe's collection of indoor-trained orange and pomegranate trees, some of them four hundred years old, from Neuilly.

The side areas of the naves were divided into 'Courts'— Greek, Roman, Graeco-Roman, Egyptian, Moorish, Medieval, Renaissance—displaying the art and architecture of the different eras or localities mostly in the form of plaster reproductions. In the Moorish court for example, the façade of the Alhambra was faithfully reproduced; huge statues, sphinxes and obelisks in the Egyptian court brought the names of Karnak, Dendera and Abu Simbel to life whilst leaving unanswered the question of how the inaccessible Abu Simbel rock carvings were accurately reproduced to such a scale at such a time; the Grecian court was modelled on the lines of a Temple of Jupiter adorned both with real and reproduction statuary; in the Medieval court the visitor could study French royal tombs or architectural details of Salisbury or Wells cathedrals. In addition to these courts the new south transept housed a collection of modern statuary and early keyboard instruments whilst the galleries were used for the display of more than five hundred portrait busts, many from the hands of the once-admired and long-forgotten Baron Marochetti.

The attempt to combine instruction with amusement was not confined to the interior of the Palace, and in the lower part of the grounds palæontology was represented, in the words of Violet Markham, by :

> ... a series, created under Professor Owen's personal direction, of those vast and unpleasant animals that existed on our planet, fortunately before man had made his appearance. Specimens of the Iguanadon, the Plesiosaurus, the Pterodactyl and other mercifully extinct brutes (formerly known to the Weald of Kent and Sussex) sported on islands specially arranged for them. A dinner-party of twenty-one people was held in the body of one of these monsters, and from the skull Professor Owen delivered a stirring address on the labours of geologists.

Plaster reproductions of architectural details or cement representations of the better-dead might be dismissed by late twentieth-century critics as boring or bizarre—or both, but the serious side of the Crystal Palace displays filled a need at a time when the crowded collections of the British Museum were still piled hugger-mugger in their old cramped quarters. The Natural History and Science Museums, the Victoria and Albert, the Wallace Collection and similar displays simply did not exist. Similarly, despite some acoustic shortcomings the great concert hall filled a gap which music-lovers had long deplored, while the lighter side of the attractions, the balloon ascents and the tight-rope walking, the restaurants and gardens, the fountains and fireworks were enormously attractive. So attractive indeed as to inspire imitation by Lord Brougham who laid the foundation stone of the 'Palace of the People' at Muswell Hill in 1862. This Palace, 'Ally-Pally' to millions and the Alexandra Palace to the few who recall that it was named in honour of the Prince of Wales's bride, was sponsored by the Great Northern Palace Company which was no more than the Great Northern Railway Company under another hat; it marks the first example of a railway company financing a public recreation resort.

For the first thirty years of its Sydenham life the Crystal Palace was extremely popular and out-ranked the Tower of London or Madame Tussaud's as a magnet for foreign visitors, but its crippled finances were a source of perpetual worry to the Directors. As early as September 1852 the original half-million of capital had to be doubled and by the time the Palace was reopened £1,350,000 had been spent. This was a staggering sum by 1854 standards and most of it was raised by mortgages and loans the interest on which left a perilously narrow margin of the Company's income for maintenance and repairs. A severe injury was inflicted on the Palace when the Evangelicals, the Lord's Day Observance Society and similar bodies of self-righteous guardians of other people's morals contrived to get all places of public entertainment closed on Sundays—except for religious meetings or concerts of sacred music. Lord Shaftesbury was closely associated with this move and it is a sad irony that the man who had done so much to ease the sufferings of the labouring poor now made a mockery of their one day of leisure. The idea that the Crystal and Alexandra Palaces should be for 'the people' was firmly squashed and the incomes of the buildings severely reduced. In 1866 fire broke out in the north transept and the Company had neither the spirit nor the cash to rebuild it. For the rest of its life the truncated limb of the Palace bore witness to moral myopia and financial stringency.

10 The Profit

The profit from the Exhibition in the Crystal Palace, £186,000, seems a mere trifle 125 years later, but the good which flowed from it could not now be bought for a fortune. The Royal Commission for the Exhibition of 1851 is still active and administers a large income for the benefit of a number of institutions, museums and learned bodies which were either non-existent or of small account in 1851.

As always, the suggestions put forward for spending the money were numerous and sometimes absurd. After the decision to remove the Crystal Palace from Hyde Park had been made, a supplementary charter was granted to the Commissioners empowering them to dispose of the money as they thought fit for the benefit of the nation by furthering the causes of science and art, and it was thanks to Prince Albert, ably seconded by Henry Cole and a handful of other far-sighted public figures, that it was well spent.

Plaintive suggestions from some of the bodies for the return of some of the funds they had subscribed when the Exhibition was in low water were predictably ignored and, inevitably, there was a sycophantic clamour to raise a memorial to Prince Albert which he most firmly resisted. He wrote to Lord Granville:

I can only say with perfect absence of humbug that I

would much rather not be made the prominent feature of such a monument ... as it would disturb my quiet rides up Rotten Row to see my own face staring at me; and if (as is very likely) it became an artistic monstrosity, like most of our monuments, it would upset my equanimity to be permanently laughed at and ridiculed in effigy.... [It were better] to mark the corners of the building site by permanent stones with inscriptions ... and give the surplus money to the erection of the Museum of Art and Science.

The line in the Prince's letter about giving the money to a Museum of Art and Science contains the clue to his hopes. Bringing Art and Science together now sounds typically Albertian in the pejorative sense which is all too often used of him; but using Art in its widest sense to include engineering, manufacturing and industry the need for a marriage with Science was urgent.

Nearly all British engineering, and consequently manufacturing, progress from the end of the seventeenth century to the culminating triumph of the Crystal Palace itself had been made empirically. Nearly all the great figures of the Industrial Revolution did what they did by rule of thumb. That they did brilliantly is undeniable but it is equally true that by 1850, as iron was about to give way to steel and the age of electricity was soon to be ushered in, it was high time for science to take a hand. As L. T. C. Rolt writes in *Victorian Engineering* :

> ... engineering was a useful art with the emphasis on art, science was a department of philosophy—'natural philosophy'—concerned with the discovery of natural laws and the formulation of theories to explain their working. From James Watt onwards, engineers had drawn freely on scientific knowledge and method—indeed their successes would otherwise have been impossible—but they mistrusted scientific theories and formulae, regarding them as no substitute for their practical

experience and using them as a check against results arrived at by their own skill and judgement and their own empirical tests. All science was then 'pure' and the phrase 'applied science' had no meaning. As late as the 1860s, one of the most eminent civil engineers of the day could contemptuously dismiss certain scientific formulae as having 'the same practical value as the weather forecasts for the year in Old Moore's Almanack'.

When we recall that fruitful eighteenth-century collaboration between engineers, industrialists and scientists exemplified by the Lunar Society, and similar bodies in London and Edinburgh; when we realize that the subsequent period did not lack British scientists as brilliant in their own fields as were their engineer contemporaries, this contempt for scientific knowledge seems unaccountable. It was probably due to an invidious comparison that was drawn between Britain and France.

In the last decades of the eighteenth century, France had led the world in scientific knowledge and in the application of scientific theory to engineering. Yet British engineers had far outstripped France in technical innovation within the space of a few decades. That the reason was largely political and economic; that the British engineer and industrialist operated in conditions of freedom unknown in France and enjoyed a unique export trade was not recognized, and Britain's proud position as the workshop of the world was attributed to some mysterious, innate engineering genius peculiar to the British. While others wasted their time poring over calculations, theories and formulae, the British engineer, by sheer talent and inspiration, had produced a better job. This myth would have unfortunate effects.

The danger in the myth grew greater as America and Germany, particularly the latter, forged ahead after 1860 with industrial expansion coupled with full co-operation from their scientific establishments which, again particularly in Germany, were better-educated and better-organized than their British counterparts. The dangers were apparent to the Prince who was also aware of another weakness in the British system—the rabid dislike of centralization. The mildest degree of government intervention was resisted with fanatical energy by all bodies from the most modest parish council to the most influential learned society.

The Prince set out the first tentative outline of his scheme in a memorandum in August 1851:

> In contrast with France and its Central School of Arts and Manufactures I find that in England the separate pursuits of industry are represented by a variety of public societies struggling for existence unconnected with each other, and either unprovided with suitable locations or exhausting in providing them the funds which should be applied to the promotion of their respective objects. Could not such societies, or most of them, containing as they do all that this country possesses of talent and experience in these branches, be induced to unite in this institution, reserving to each its individuality and self-supporting and self-maintaining character, but bringing them together under a common roof.

To put flesh on this skeleton it was proposed that the Commissioners should buy from Baron de Villars an estate of nearly fifty acres stretching southward from Kensington Gore, together with some smaller parcels of land, to use part of the area for private houses to provide income and to establish on the remainder four great new teaching institutions representing the four main divisions of the exhibition: Raw materials and geology, Machinery, Manufactures and the Plastic Arts. Prince Albert and his colleagues must soon have realized that grouping all 'under a common roof' would be too much for the centralization-hating English to stomach, but it was proposed that in addition to the four new bodies the existing learned societies might also be brought together into one great institution on the new site, with arrangements for all the contributors to the Exhibition to be life members.

Understandably enough, this plan was not developed without change and without opposition, and the notion of grouping together the existing learned societies was the first to go as even the mildest form of association or combining under the aegis of a central body was as truly shocking to the mid-Victorian ethos as financial dishonesty. Indeed, the Prince himself did not wish the centralization to be all-embracing and he wrote—to the Prime Minister—of the oldest of all the learned societies, the august Royal Society:

> To give [any part of] the surplus away in order to provide with better accommodation a Society which, as at present constituted, has forfeited the sympathy of the generality of the public by its lethargic state and exclusive principles, cannot, I am sure, be thought of for a moment.

The Government favoured the scheme in principle and were prepared to match the Commission's expenditure pound for pound on mortgage until it could be self-supporting. As the plan was bound to create controversy and opposition it was thought best to negotiate for the land secretly in order to present that part of the business as a *fait accompli*, otherwise the opportunity to buy the land might be lost. Governments are often justly accused of being too secretive, but that they were right on this occasion is shown by the fact that a long-established myth in anti-Albert circles, still believed by many, is that the Prince filched part of the Exhibition profits to buy himself land in South Kensington. If this could be believed after the transaction it is clear how great a clamour would have been raised against it at the time, and so the secrecy may be condoned. Fortunately the Chancellor of the Exchequer of the day, Benjamin Disraeli, was as sympathetic and helpful as, a little later, William

Gladstone, in the same office, was obstructive.

The Villars estate was bought for £150,000, and the sale of the Crystal Palace to the new company provided about half that sum. The promised Government backing enabled the Commissioners to buy additional land to the south of the Villars estate to make the total 'exhibition site' 87 acres. Of these, 17 acres were used for good quality, large, private houses, 40 acres were ultimately bought by the Government at very low prices for public use, principally for museums etc., and the remaining 12 acres were leased to educational and scientific bodies at nominal rents.

The income from the estate and other investments by the Commissioners provided means to help the following institutions to settle and flourish on the site : the Royal College of Arts, Royal School of Mines, Royal College of Science, City and Guilds College, Royal College of Music, the Imperial Institute, the Science Museum, the Victoria and Albert Museum and the Natural History Museum which includes the Geological Museum. The Commission also finances numerous scholarships and foundations. The existing independent learned societies were, as foreseen, reluctant to settle under the Royal Commission's wing, but the Physical Society, the Royal Geographical Society and the Royal College of Organists finally did so.

None of this happened overnight, of course, and most of it was done after Prince Albert's death in 1862, but if his spirit lives anywhere it is in that territory bounded by Kensington Road and Hyde Park to the north, Brompton and Cromwell Roads to the south, Exhibition Road on the east and Queen's Gate on the west. Many of the institutions which have sprung up on the site have grown out of all recognition. Nor do their names always do justice to their activities : the dull-sounding School of Mines, for example, teaches mining theory and practice, metallurgy, geology, oil technology, chemistry in relation to agriculture, botany and zoology in relation to geology as well as doing practical research work on mining safety and keeping historical records. Similarly the simple name of the City and Guilds

College hides the functions of a body which would qualify for the title of the Royal College of Engineering and Technology, with all that that implies in an industrial society.

In *1851 and the Crystal Palace* Christopher Hobhouse wrote of the Prince's scheme as expressed through the Royal Commission:

> ... having explored every avenue and listened to every suggestion [they] came to the staggering conclusion that London was insufficiently provided with museums and galleries and that their best plan was to lay out their funds ... in order that more museums and galleries might be built.

In this passage Mr Hobhouse's usual perspicacity deserted him. Though vital to the plan the museums at South Kensington were always regarded by the originators as complementary to the schools of engineering, painting, music, and the other bodies which they set up in close proximity, not only to propagate their own branches of learning but to bridge the gap between science and art. Also, the London of 1852 *was* insufficiently provided with museums and galleries, disgracefully so by comparison with some other capitals, and the success of the Crystal Palace Exhibition had shown how eager the public were to widen their horizons.

In 1852 the British Museum itself was still five years away from the completion of its present quarters (doubled in size since then and again inadequate), and cramped into Montague House which was almost literally on the point of collapse from the sheer weight of objects crammed into it hugger mugger. Sir Hans Sloane's original collection had been swamped by later acquisitions from George III's collection of scientific instruments and his library, as well as ethnological specimens, fossils, paintings and the rest, with many exhibits, such as the Elgin Marbles, too heavy to be brought into the old building and others stored out of sight in a variety of attics and cellars. Apart from the privileged few who had access to private collections, to the Royal

Academy's Summer Exhibition or the Water Colour Society's annual show there were no places for the public to look at the nation's pictures. Antique collecting and investigation were then a matter of learned gentlemen poking into the ruins of Herculaneum or Karnak, and old furniture, clocks, tapestries, enamels, ceramics, jewellery were nowhere available for study; and apart from a small and overcrowded collection at the Patent Office scientific and engineering objects also had no place.

All these wants were gradually filled in the half-century after the Crystal Palace was built, and under the modest title of Secretary to the Department of Art and Science Henry Cole was one of the principal creators of the edifice Prince Albert had planned. He had already played an important part in setting up the Government Schools of Design which expanded into the constituent parts of the Imperial College of Science. Towards the end of his career, being responsible for both Science and Art, Cole's zeal for centralization, modest though it was by modern standards, ranged some of the scientists against him; he fell into some political disfavour consequently and was retired in 1875, aged sixty-seven, with a consolatory knighthood.

During the quarter-century following the Great Exhibition Cole's first occupation was with the South Kensington Museum, now the Victoria and Albert, from which the scientific collection was not divorced until 1884, two years after Cole's death. The growth of the South Kensington Museum from its modest start on the first floor of Marlborough House (under the name of the Museum of Manufactures) to its removal to its first Kensington home in 1857 and its subsequent growth to its present stature, with its offshoots at Apsley House, Ham and Bethnal Green, cannot be dealt with here. One of Cole's many innovations has survived as a part of general museum administration policy which nobody now challenges; this is the use of the central collections as a reservoir to supply loan exhibitions in the provinces.

One of Cole's tenets now finds much less favour. Although

he was dedicated to the ideal of giving ordinary men and women the chance to enjoy beautiful and interesting things previously reserved for the rich, Cole was a firm believer in charging for admission. In countless public speeches and official reports Cole urged the propriety of charging nominal fees, not with the object of raising money but in order to sharpen appreciation. He considered a penny the proper charge for ordinary admissions but advocated charging higher prices, sixpence or even a shilling, on certain days or times to give serious students more space and quiet in which to work. Like the Prince Consort and Queen Victoria he was a fierce opponent of Sunday closing but this was a battle he could not win.

It was the need to keep museums from becoming frowsty, boring, overcrowded collections of miscellanea which dictated constant change and enlargement, with the division of Natural History from the British Museum, of the Science Department from the South Kensington Museum and so on. During the last thirty years a great wave of new vigour and new ideas has swept through the national museums and galleries with salutary effects. Less than forty years ago Christopher Hobhouse could write with some truth of the South Kensington complex:

> Here, on these barren acres, nobody lives, nobody loves, nobody dies. Here, on the one side, are all the trumpery flotsam of learning, stuffed mammals and fossils, stuck into glass cases and labelled in the hope of filling some vacant mind. And here, on the other side, are some of the loveliest things on earth, whole rooms of English furniture, and the Raphael cartoons, and Pellé's bust of Charles the Second—here they are snatched from the hands of private men, sterilized, caged together in tasteless surfeit, imprisoned without hope of release. Here too, perhaps saddest of all, is a great staff of experts— unhappy custodians, bound by hated necessity to the prisoners of their great seraglio, yet pleased with a gloating pleasure that other men cannot get near them

to enjoy them. From beyond their glass cages a few German and Japanese students of all ages come and blink through their spectacles at them and go away again, having added one more piece of information to the silly pile....

No more than mildly unjust when it was written this diatribe now seems almost absurd. There is nothing sterile about the collections to which millions go for pleasure and often leave with profit. C. R. Fay's summing up in *The Palace of Industry, 1851,* paints a truer picture than Hobhouse:

... the estate, we see, presents a peculiar jumble of planning and accretion. Yet behind it all we can still see the grand design of Prince Albert and Henry Cole and give credit to the profits of the Great Exhibition which made it possible. And if we look further with the eye of imagination, can we not see behind the Victorian buildings of South Kensington the shining glass structure of the original Palace ... and the millions from all countries who came to visit and admire?

11 The Loss

The fear of fire had not been treated lightly when it had been voiced during the construction of the Crystal Palace in Hyde Park. Paxton had assuaged anxiety to some extent by publicizing the ample unobstructed exits and the twenty-five fire points in the building, each served by a nine-inch main and manned by specially-trained sappers, as the private soldiers in the Corps of Royal Engineers were still called.

To the lay mind a glass and iron building sounded reassuringly fire-proof, but the experts knew better, and knew how much wood was used in the construction and could visualize all manner of flammable materials, from silk to beeswax, in the exhibits. With his turn of mind and from his work as a Commissioner of Records who had contributed much to the fire safety aspects of design in the new Record Office, Henry Cole was something of an authority on precautions against fire. Rather curiously, in the eyes of the 1970s, he came out strongly against central heating, either by hot-water radiators or hot-air ducts, in the Public Record Office building and urged the greater safety of properly guarded open fires. He was probably influenced by the belief that the fire which destroyed the old Houses of Parliament was started by an overheated flue in the hot-air system arising from the

over-zealous stoking of a furnace with several centuries'
accumulation of Exchequer tally-sticks.

As part of his duties on the Executive Committee Cole
wrote a Report for the Commissioners on the '. . . Security of
the Building from Fire'. As the principal enemy of safety
from fire is found in large enclosed areas with no inner sub-
divisions to confine outbreaks and minimize draught, this
report started rather despondently :

> In the estimate of the probable cost of the Exhibition,
> I have assumed that the Commissioners, in declaring
> that the building will be fire-proof, intend the term
> 'fire-proof' to be interpreted in a comparative, rather
> than a positive sense, and I ventured on making this
> assumption, because the inquiries into the best means
> of making a building fire-proof, which it has been my
> duty to prosecute for some years past ... in reference
> to the Public Record Office, have led me to the con-
> clusion that a building, fire-proof in a strict sense, would
> not only be far too costly for the object proposed, but
> would be, in the very nature of its construction, unsuit-
> able for the purposes of the Exhibition.

Having outlined the precautions taken in the Record Office
and discussed the folly of covering wood with metal, Henry
Cole concluded :

> The conditions of the building for the Exhibition are
> that it is to be temporary, that it must not be too costly,
> and that the chambers in it must be spacious. ... But
> as these conditions appear to be incompatible with
> positive 'fire-proofedness', and as I have reason to
> believe that no species of building possible under
> the circumstances, would sensibly affect the *rate of
> insurance*—an infallible gauge of security—I submit
> that the security from fire should be obtained by vigilant
> watching, and efficient preparations to extinguish fire,
> if it should unfortunately happen, and that the materials

and mode of construction ought therefore to be selected solely for their fitness and economy.

This report was actually written before Paxton's design was accepted but the same criteria applied, and when the Exhibition was over Cole was able to write that, thanks to the 'vigilant watching', the only fire had been a matter of some cotton waste smouldering in a rubbish bin. The 'no smoking' rule was imposed partly to reduce the fire hazard, and for the same reason no cooking was allowed on the premises. The refreshment rooms served only cold food and the hot drinks and soups were heated by steam from the smaller of the external boiler houses. Also, only enough artificial light was needed to allow the night-duty policemen and sappers to patrol the building at night.

Conditions were very much less satisfactory at Sydenham. The building had to be adequately, even brilliantly, lit at night and many thousands of gas lamps were installed. These were replaced by an electric lighting installation in 1891, but it is probable that this early installation itself became something of a fire hazard as it grew old. The extensive 'dining saloons' required extensive kitchens with gas and coal ranges, and most parts of the building were warmed by a hot-water circulating system with its furnaces and boilers in the basement. Contemporary reports are silent about a possible no smoking rule, but contemporary engravings show cigar-smoking gentlemen dining at candle-lit tables. In one respect the 'new' Crystal Palace was apparently less of a fire hazard than the original buildings as it was less open, but 'apparently' is the operative word as many of the sub-divisions were without ceilings and were too often composed of thin tongued-and-grooved boarding or other flammable stuff. Also the Corps of Royal Engineers no longer provided a day and night guard of well-trained sappers to man the fire points scattered through the building. The fire which destroyed the north transept on 30 December 1866 showed how quickly a fire could get out of control, though in fairness it must be said that an unexpectedly early hard frost had reduced the water supply.

As the fortunes of the Crystal Palace declined so the fire hazard increased because more spaces were divided off and sub-let as fortune-telling booths, souvenir stalls or lecture rooms. That the fortunes were declining became apparent before the end of the century when the typically late-Victorian euphemism of 'seedy' became sadly applicable to the mid-Victorian masterpiece. Those who had known the Crystal Palace in Hyde Park, or during its first vigorous years at Sydenham, now felt towards it rather as to a once-prosperous and sprightly relative to whom they ought to pay a duty visit in the geriatric ward.

Both Queen Victoria grappling with the Boer War ('These news are terrible'), and the Crystal Palace grappling with rising costs and dwindling income had to face the unpalatable fact that their day was done. In 1851 Great Britain had been producing more coal and iron than France, Germany and America put together, had owned more than half the world's shipping and had faced negligible competition industrially as France was still relatively backward in manufacturing, America had almost no export trade except of raw materials and Italy and Germany were still random collections of petty sovereign states. In 1851 almost the only anxiety the Queen had felt from Germany had been a matter of personal animosity towards her old Uncle Ernest, King of Hanover, because of his dislike of Albert and his protectionist policies. But by 1900 the sabre-rattling antics of her neurotic grandson Wilhelm II, Kaiser of a mighty united German Empire, were matters of real concern, and both German and American industry were taking large bites out of England's former supremacy. The difficulty of managing too large an empire was becoming apparent as were the disadvantages of having been first in so many fields —later comers were able to build up new industries without risk of disruption to elder ones. The Crystal Palace had been conceived as the temple of peace and progress, but peace was shattered and there were those who warned that progress was a false god.

The *fin-de-siècle* generation had new amusements. One may be sure that in the seventies a newly-married Mr Pooter would have relished a day at the Crystal Palace with Carrie on his arm, but one may be equally certain that the brash and graceless Lupin Pooter in the nineties would have scorned it as dull and old-fashioned. With the bicycle craze in full flood, electric light and the telephone burgeoning on every side, with the cinematograph and the motor car emerging from the experimental stage, a 'spin in the country' and a visit to the music hall were more to the taste of the young than a train journey to Sydenham and a decorous concert under the shadow of the great organ, followed by a walk in the crumbling gardens where the fountains no longer played and the antediluvian monsters seemed merely shabby and ridiculous in their weed-choked lakes.

The burden of maintenance weighed heavily on the Crystal Palace Company. The building designed for six months' use could only be kept permanently sound by constant painting, and the money was never quite enough to ensure that the painting was ever properly finished. The use of unseasoned timber in the guttering had caused minor trouble when the building was new, but as it passed its half-century neglected paintwork in the roof allowed the putty to crack, the panes to slip and the rainwater to come in. The need for extensive repairs to the central transept in 1890 underlined the fact that all those miles of Paxton gutter, shaped ridge-beams and special glazing bars should have been of galvanized iron after all—and the once-pure air of Sydenham was now so laden with sulphuric-acid gas that the frilly cornices of sheet zinc crumbled at a touch if they were left unpainted.

By selling almost a third of the land for building the Company held disaster at bay for a time, but by 1909 the game was up and a Receiver was appointed. This had the inevitable result that many who had not given the old place a thought for a quarter of a century now protested at the notion of the whole estate being sold for building land and the Palace broken up for scrap. Business, such as it was,

was carried on by the Receiver until 1911 when the Court of Chancery ordered the sale of the entire property which was then valued at £230,000. Some of the contents had already been dispersed when Lord Plymouth raised the necessary money, and the Lord Mayor, on behalf of the City of London, set up a trust fund to repay him and to save the building and gardens for the nation.

During the first two and a half years after this reprieve the Palace continued to attract visitors in fair numbers. It might have been a far cry from Handel festivals to baby shows and revivalist meetings but at least the place was not dead, even if a little curtained-off pierrot show and rows of penny-in-the-slot machines made strange bedfellows for reproduction Grecian statuary and medieval architecture. Perhaps even more incongruous was the use of a small part of the building for the world's first motor museum. This was assembled by Mr Edmund Dangerfield, the Proprietor of *The Motor*, who foresaw that people would one day cherish what his contemporaries saw as worthless scrap.

During the 1914-18 war the Crystal Palace was used as a naval barracks, which did it little good. The more easily movable contents, including Dangerfield's early motor cars, were garaged elsewhere, and the neglected building peeled and leaked worse than ever. Immediately the war was over, however, the Trustees, reinvigorated with fresh funds from the city, set about the mammoth task of restoration with such a will that the King and Queen were able to reopen the place to the public in June 1920.

For sixteen years, under the enthusiastic hand of Sir Henry Buckland, the work went on and the Palace enjoyed a new lease of life. It was a different, more rumbustious, out-of-doors life than before. The Historical Courts had lost their charm and that migratory bore—as Christopher Hobhouse calls it—the Imperial War Museum, was for a time housed in the building Prince Albert had seen as a temple of peace, before being moved on to other quarters and finally coming to rest, fittingly enough, in the former lunatic asylum of Bedlam. Where Clara Novello's voice had seemed likely to shatter the glass and the music-lovers had assembled for Sunday concerts of 'sacred' music, the Four Square Gospellers met for communal baptism in a heated tank and part of one of the side aisles had been turned into an aviary for parrots.

Where the Victorian ladies and gentlemen had paraded up and down the terraces overlooking Paxton's garden, pausing perhaps to watch a balloon ascent by one of the Spencer family or Blondin walking the tight-rope stretched high between the terraces on the southern slope (not between the water towers as tradition asserts), were ice cream stalls and roundabouts. The cinder track used for bicycle and motor-tricycle races in the late 1890s was now devoted to dirt-track riding. The Handel festivals were not revived but the Foden Steam Waggon Company's brass band won the annual contest with monotonous regularity. Though the restoration of the water displays and lakes was never completed, the gardens, though smaller and cut up by sports arenas and sideshows, regained much of their former splendour, and many of the statues, including eight tons of marble representing Joseph Paxton, were bought back and replaced on their pedestals.

By 1936, though there was still much to do and the workmen never stopped hammering, repairing and painting, most of the neglect had been made good and attendance had gone up to about one million visitors a year; this yielded about £80,000 and a useful reserve fund was accumulating. Sir Henry Buckland and the trustees may well have begun to think of centenary celebrations, but on the night of 30 November 1936 fire broke out in the administrative offices. Sir Henry, who lived nearby, saw the glow as he returned from posting a letter. Some workmen were trying to deal with the blaze and had already telephoned the fire brigade, but by the time Sir Henry had warned the members of an orchestra (some of whom lost their motor cars) practising in the concert hall things looked very serious. There was a strong wind blowing from the south-west and the fire was perilously near the end wall of the transept; once the glass or boarded panels gave way and admitted the gale the fire would be uncontrollable.

Despite the efforts of fire brigades from all over south London, deploying a total of eighty-nine engines, it was soon apparent they could save nothing but the low level station and the water towers, which, had they been full, might have provided some relief. At the height of the blaze, as the glass melted and ran down the terraces and the iron frame buckled in the heat, the flames rose three hundred feet. Of those among the millions who watched, from as far away as the hills above Brighton, many must have remembered sadly that the Crystal Palace had long been famous for its firework displays.

Others have strange but strong memories of a myth, for a legend has become firmly established that the fire was deliberate, and not merely the work of an arsonist but a deliberate act by Government for a particular purpose. The most recent version of this legend was heard in a Hampshire public house in November 1973 where the subject of the Crystal Palace fire happened to crop up. The landlord, a self-assertive elderly cockney, claimed to have been living near by and to have stood on Anerley Hill, coughing in the smoke and fumes, half-hoping and half-fearing the south tower would fall. The fire was, he said, a deliberate act ordered by the Government and executed by the soldiers who were billeted in the Palace at the time. The Royal Engineers, he said, had been trying to make the great building less conspicuous from the air by coating the whole structure with paint in camouflage patterns. Finding the task impossible and the building such a beacon to guide German bombers to London, the Government had ordered its destruction. When it was gently pointed out that the fire occurred in 1936 and not during the war the little man grew irate. 'I was there,' he shouted. 'I tell you I was there; are you calling me a liar? I tell you I was there and it was during the battle of Britain; and when they realized they couldn't camelflarge it they burnt the bleeding thing down—I was bloody there I tell you. After all,' he concluded, 'stands to reason they'd 'ave to take it down doesn't it, because it was put up by Queen Victoria's German 'usband.'

After so splendid a *non sequitur* there seems no more to be said about the mid-Victorian masterpiece.

Extracts from Henry Cole's Memoirs

One of the first acts of the Royal Commission was to appoint a Building Committee on the 24th January, 1850. Besides the Duke of Buccleuch and the Earl of Ellesmere, it was composed of three architects and three civil engineers all having attained eminent positions. The architects were Mr Barry, R.A. (afterwards Sir Charles), Mr Cockerell, R.A., and Mr Donaldson. The engineers were Mr Brunel, Mr W. Cubitt (afterwards Sir William), and Mr Robert Stephenson. Mr Joseph Locke, M.P. was not one, and he never forgave the omission, but visited his indignation on South Kensington and all its offspring. This Committee was too numerous and too strong to be workable. It again illustrated the old proverb of 'too many cooks'. Art and Science did *not* work together, and throughout were opposed to the very end. Any *one* of the six could have done the work well, acting on his own responsibility. But the whole nearly wrecked the Exhibition by dispute and delay, and after five months produced an impracticable plan, which was superseded by the glasshouse of a gardener, a man of genius, but no architect or engineer.

On the 21st February the Building Committee reported to the Commission in favour of the site on the south side of Hyde Park which had already been recommended when the idea was started in the preceding year, and proposed that there should be a public competition 'for suggestions as to the general arrangements ... of the building etc.' ... The plans were to be sent in on or before the 8th of April. ... The Committee reported on the 9th of May that they had arrived 'at the unanimous conclusion that able and admirable as many of them appeared to be, there was yet no single one so accordant with the peculiar objects in view, either in principle or details of its arrangement, as to warrant us in recommending its adoption.' And they submitted a design of their own, in which they recommended '*some striking feature to exemplify the present state of the science of construction in this country.*' This was done on the advice of Mr Brunel. The Committee on the 11th July reported that they had received tenders from nineteen persons; they had examined the various tenders and considered what reductions might be made by omitting the dome and other accessories, not absolutely required, and without committing themselves to any precise sum, they believed that the whole building might be constructed and removed for something under £100,000. They could not at that time report more precisely. They noticed that Mr Paxton had proposed a building of iron and glass, and that there did not appear to be any economy in this plan; on the contrary, the cost would appear likely to exceed by nearly ten per cent that of the ordinary construction proposed by the Committee. After a delay of nearly five precious months the work of the Building Committee was abortive, as their ultimate adoption of Paxton's plan proved it to be. The 'striking feature' was to have been a dome 200 feet high, and nineteen millions of bricks were to have been used in Hyde Park. It was manifestly impracticable, and was condemned by the public. The design and building were repudiated even by the members of the Committee individually. I sat next to Mr Barry under the Gallery in the House of Commons on the 4th July, 1850, when the use of Hyde Park was discussed and he said, 'I have had nothing to do with the design, and repudiate it.'

The Prince was sorely troubled at this period. He wrote to Baron Stockmar: 'The Exhibition is now attacked furiously by *The Times*, and the House of Commons is going to drive us out of the park. There is immense excitement on the subject. If we are driven out of the park, the work is done for! Never was anything so foolish. ... *The Times*, has all at once made a set against me and the Exhibition ... we are to pack out of London with our nuisance to the Isle of Dogs....'

At this crisis, when only three tenders were received, and nothing was actually settled about the building, Lord Granville and Col. Reid gave me permission to go to Liverpool, Manchester and Birmingham to seek for other tenders, if possible, below the three received. So I started by night mail, 29th June. At Liverpool, Mr W. Rathbone (a great friend of the Penny Postage* and the Exhibition) took me to Mr S. and Mr A. Holmes, but I obtained no hope that they would tender. At Manchester, Mr Salis Schwabe, a warm friend of R. Cobden, introduced me to Mr Bellhouse who, after two hours' consideration, declined to tender. I then went to Birmingham, called at Fox & Henderson's Works at Smethwick, and the following are notes made at the time. 'Mr Fox away, Found Mr Henderson only, who was prepared to tender for the plan according to Paxton's design. Suggested he should tender for the [*Official*] plan duly economized, also to take the risk. He advised my remaining to see his partner. Went over his works with Mr Cowper. Mr Fox came in the evening by express from London. We all met at the Queen's Hotel. Fox said it would be hardly possible to erect the Committee's plan in time. ... Euston took 20,000,000 bricks and five months to lay; there would be 3,000 cubic yards of water to evaporate. 32oz. glass could not be made in the time [*for Paxton's plan*], because it must be annealed before it is cut. Stayed till half-past twelve discussing. Both agreed to tender in three ways.' 4th July 1850,—'Called on Mr Lascelles and Thomson to get signatures to petition against change of site. Saw Cobden, rode round the Park to find out the number of householders who would be damnified, if at all. Prepared paper on amount of damage to residents; took it to Lord Granville; said he thought it very good and ... wished Mr Labouchere to have a copy. At the Commons under the Gallery during debate on the Exhibition site. ... Called at Buckingham Palace to tell result; Prince said he would see me; up to his private room. He was very nervous; said it had never entered his head that anyone would object. If the site had not been affirmed he was prepared to give up the Exhibition; it was "like asking your friends to your flower garden and putting them among the cabbages." The death of Sir R. Peel was horrible ... called on old Dilke who advised me not to resign.' July 5th 1850,—'J. Bell the sculptor called to hear fate of division on the site—162 for to 47 against. At Palace Yard, Reid (who had the boldness of a lion with the timidity of a hare),

* It will occasion no surprise to the reader to learn that Henry Cole had been an active campaigner for the penny post, and had played an important part in organizing its introduction.

said to me, "Henceforth, we must not be the focus of any agitation. Committees must not be asked by *us* to support the Commission about the site or anything else. Mayors of Birmingham or Bradford must do it." Lord Overstone came to deplore the risks which a contractor or guarantor would run—Queen's or Prince's death, foreign war, etc.'

[*The record then continues with the account of Cole's negotiations with guarantors, culminating in Sir Morton Peto's undertaking on behalf of himself and friends to guarantee or advance £50,000 pour encourager les autres. On Cole's urging, Morton Peto put his offer on record in a letter to Prince Albert's private secretary. The account then continues:*]

The letter was sent the same evening and great joy it gave the Prince. It started the guarantee brilliantly, and before long about £350,000 were subscribed. . . .

On the 15th of July 1850, I called at Buckingham Palace on Colonel Grey (who had succeeded Colonel Phipps as Private Secretary) I take the following notes from my diary: 'The Prince came into Grey's room, and, as his manner often was, sat upon the table. I related the details of Peto's guarantee. The Prince applauded it "as a most useful thing in having stirred up others!" He said, "Now was the time for work, it was not plans that were wanted." . . . I told the Prince candidly "my opinion of the state of the present arrangements, delay, difficulty, cost etc." The Prince asked, "What is being done about the catalogues?" and then went on to say, "Playfair would see to the Collection well, but who the arrangement of the exhibits?" He did not know who the man was who was to bring the thing together.' The Prince left and I had some further talk with Colonel Grey, and I told him I had thought of resigning to make things easier. Grey strongly dissuaded me from thinking about it, and I was led on to saying I would not shrink from the work if *officially* charged with the arrangement of exhibits, and he said he would promote it.

The same day the Commissioners agreed to put aside the brick plan of the Building Committee, for the execution of which Mr Brassey tendered for £81,141, and virtually to adopt Paxton's, for which Messrs Fox and Henderson tendered at £79,800, and they undertook to execute it, including the semi-cylindrical roof . . . by the 1st January 1851. . . . Before the building was completed the cost had mounted up to £107,780, and finally £142,780 were paid but this included an extra sum of £35,000 to the contractors 'taking into consideration the important services of Messrs Fox and Henderson, the unprecedented character of the undertaking, the shortness of time allowed for its completion, and the energy and liberality with which the contractors had laboured to meet the wishes of the Commission.'

[*In a later passage in his account Henry Cole wrote of some of the opposition he and his colleagues encountered, which he concluded as follows:*]

After the first scare had subsided, and Paxton's building was actually begun, there arose a fear that the building would not stand, but be thrown down like a pack of cards. Mr Airy, the Astronomer-Royal, wrote a pamphlet in which he demonstrated that it *must* come down. Like Dr Lardner's prophecy that no steamer would ever be able to cross the Atlantic,* Airy's prophecy must always remain as a caution against the utterance of assertions as arrogant in theoretical science, as papal dogmatism is in theological belief.

[*In a lecture on the International Results of the Exhibition Henry Cole referred to the awards of the coveted Council Medals:*]

If we look down the list of 164 Council Medals, and the objects to which they were awarded, I confess it seems to me there is but *one* object with which the world became acquainted for the first time, and that as a direct result of the Exhibition. ... That solitary one, which no one was acquainted with was the building itself which Paxton suggested. The Exhibition has taught the world how to roof in great spaces; how to build with glass and iron in a way never done before.... The one material thing absolutely necessary for an international exhibition was an adequate building to be erected in six months. And after many galvanic struggles to get it one was obtained. Nothing very novel in iron columns resting on concrete foundations,—nothing novel in Paxton gutters, which half a dozen persons claim to have invented ... but something very novel in covering twenty acres with glass as an exhibiting room, a feat the world had not seen performed before. I look upon this building as one of great

* Dr Dionysius Lardner's dogmatic assertion that 'the notion that a vessel might cross the Atlantic Ocean by the power of steam alone is utterly chimerical', was uttered only a few weeks before the *Sirius* and the *Great Western* proved him wrong.

importance ... but even in the material Glasshouse, as in the possibility of an International Exhibition, Sir Robert Peel appears as an agent. Had the excise duties on glass still remained, it is certain we could not have had the Crystal Palace.

APPENDIX B

Punch's comments on the fate of the *Crystal Palace*

Shall the Crystal Palace Stand? Are we to take to ourselves the closing ceremonies of the Exhibition as sad, dull presages of the doom of the wondrous fabric itself—a doom resolved upon, and relentlessly pursued by the stern wisdom of the great Pan* of the woods and forests? If so, most pertinently, most admir- ably, were those ceremonies ordered: for the very genius of dumpishness, of sullen wilfulness, presided on the Saturday [*the last public day*], and on the final Wednesday. Not a man appeared in the lac-a-daisical pageant, not one, from the prince to the bishop, but dulness marked him for her own. Authority seemed to be remorseful of the jocund bearing held on the 1st of May; and therefore did a sort of dropjaw penance on the 15th of October. Hum-drum was paramount! And the skies sym- pathized with human gloom, making all as dim and comfortless without the crystal walls, as authority was dark and glumpy within. A loyal superstition attributed the wet and murky weather to the absence of the queen. Had she graced the pageant, all would have been light and *débonnaire*, her majesty, accord- ing to the cheerful faith, being a concentration of sunbeams.
But the fact is now unalterable; and let us, as sober, melan-

* The 'great Pan' in question was Lord Seymour, Minister at the head of the Department of Woods and Forests, the precursor of the pre- sent Ministry of the Environment. 'Woods and Forests' wielded great power, and Queen Victoria complained of the difficulty of having her windows cleaned as the interiors were the responsibility of the Lord Steward's department but the exteriors had to wait on the pleasure of the 'Woods and Forests'; and seldom did the twain coincide.

choly, mind-the-main-chance Britons, rejoice thereupon. We have redeemed our character—our inalienable right—of dulness. If we did not lose somewhat in unseemly gaiety on the 1st of May; have we not recovered ourselves in the substantial stupidity of the 15th of October? If we did mum and flaunt it in the spring, to the astonishment of the stranger—who wondered much at jocund Bull!—have we not returned to our national sackcloth, our characteristic ashes, in autumn? Yes; we hope we have redeemed ourselves in the doubtful opinion of the foreigner. We have every faith that the stranger will depart from our shores with the strengthened conviction, that when John Bull in authority makes up his mind to be freezingly cold, and substantially sullen, he may triumphantly compete with all the human race. There was, as the closing ceremonial was acted, one prize medal wanting—a medal with a whole pig of lead in it for the dumps. And this medal—who can doubt it?—must have been carried off by the royal commission.

And yet there may have been a kindness intended in the gloom of the ceremony; benevolence may have lurked in the doldrums of authority. The utter blankness of meaning with which the Exhibition was declared at an end, may have been studiously, yet, withal, tenderly affected to prepare us for the grand consummation of the most profound, the most triumphant, and most barbarous stupidity (spiced somewhat with wickedness), that ever made ape kind gape at mankind;—to wit, the destruction of the last wonder of the world, the marvellous fabric, that, at a glance, has won the homage of millions. Not that the sensibility, masked in coldness of authority, was all undignified by a high, patrician philosophy; stoicism that would see the crystal wonder break into nothing, like a prismatic soap bubble. Not, moreover, that Lord Seymour is to be thought the great original of official insensibility; oh, no—

'Ere wild in Woods *that* noble savage ran'

we had many and many high example of the rabid contempt of office for the wishes of the people, Lord Seymour, able as he is in his way, is only a large contributor, not an originator. However, when the Palace shall have passed away, we trust that among the statues to be raised to commemorate its once whereabouts, there will be some effigy to eternize the condescension and urbanity radiant in the head minister of woods and forests for 1851. May we propose a statue of—The Snarling Faun?

However, taking it as foolishly and wickedly determined by authority—and no less stupidly and criminally granted and accepted by the country—that the wondrous fabric shall be broken up, having served its turn, like a child's money-box— how about the reward for the inventor of the new marvel? Great was the perplexity of the royal commission, blinded and smothered by visions of bricks and mortar—no more to be got together in the appointed time than the final bricks of Babel— when Joseph Paxton shot like a sunbeam upon the darkened council. An outrolling of a sheet of paper—a few master words —and Joseph Paxton became the deliverer of his prince and his prince's magi from difficulties that threatened to be inextric- able—making for himself a world-wide renown, and leaving his name, 'like a wild-flower to his land'.

Well, Joseph Paxton at this writing, has been offered knight- hood. What beside? Knighthood may or may not be a valuable nominal property: the word, the sound, takes its worth from the estimation of its bearer. Some men may make no more account of such title than of the jingling of pebbles in a tin-pot; others may consider it still to vibrate with ravishing music. But knighthood—mere knighthood! Have we not accidental knights—knights of good luck? Royalty goes into the city; and lo! by virtue of that happy incident, two aldermen blow into knights. 'Wings at our shoulders seem to play!' On a sudden, spurs jingle at our civic heels, delighting our civic ears. Majesty makes a progress, in pelting shower, visiting Liverpool, and— for the time—sunny Manchester. And a bran fire-new knight presses the Liverpool bolster—a knight of newest print is stamped upon the cotton city. And it may be well, with our institutions, that this should be. Where the queen of beauty set her foot, flowers sprang at the touch; where Queen Victoria travels, let honours blossom. But these are honours of ceremony —*Court Circular* glories—hardly of marked account, when vouchsafed upon man whose official life is not an accident, but whose petition in the eye of mankind has been won by the inspiration and the labour of their souls. Surely, the case of Joseph Paxton is a case of 'Genius *versus* Mayors and Aldermen'. All dues paid, the Commission are encumbered with a quarter of a *million* of money. How much of this is owing to the felici- tous genius, inspired at the happiest moment, of Joseph Paxton?

Beautiful as were the contents of the glass, the glass itself was the prime glory; bearing the same relation to the things it covered, as does the shell

'——That lustre has imbibed
In the sun's palace porch, where when unyoked
His chariot wheel stands midway in the wave',

to the fish within it. Of the millions of visitors to the Exhibition, how many came to the sight, brought thither by what they had heard and read of the wonderful Crystal Palace? That Palace, dimly shown in pictures—darkly outlined in printer's ink? Displace that beautiful fabric from the mind, and in its stead place the brick-and-mortar mountain that was to have been— granting it could have been piled up by the 1st of May—and how many tens of thousands may be deducted from the millions of pilgrims who for the past five months have thronged our streets wending to Hyde Park; there, at one glance, to acknow- ledge a wonder of beauty that seemed to realize the fiction of fairy-land: a structure raised rather by the genii of Sindbad, than the materialized thought of human genius.

Why, the Chancellor of the Exchequer is, in his pride of office, a smiling debtor to Joseph Paxton. Run through the items of the increasing revenue—at last made up—and the fiscal influence of the Crystal Palace brightens in almost every numeral. All folks with commodities to sell—or sights to show —whatever was the lull for the month of May—have reaped a tenfold harvest. There can be no sulky denial of this truth; the exchequer possesses proof of it and playhouse managers, in thankful closing speeches, confess it. But leaving all this profit apart, come we to the hard, glittering fact of a quarter of a million made beneath the roof of the Crystal Palace. What, then, for the architect? Mere knighthood? Court gingerbread with *no* gilding? This will never do. Some small per-centage from that quarter of a million is as much the due of Joseph Paxton as was his day's wage to any Joseph the glazier who worked at the fabric. All England must grant this truth; and to the will of England to insist upon this application, we hopefully leave it.

Finally, shall the Crystal Palace stand? This is a question to be answered, once and for all, by the people. A certain knot of the aristocracy, strong in their faith of official sympathy towards all that is exclusive, all that is contemptuous of the masses, already rejoice in the certainty of the demolition of the five-months wonder of the world. If the people do not speak with one loud, unstammering voice, Lord Seymour and his merry men will rush to the destruction; jolly and full-blooded as the Goths rushed into Rome. And they will do Goths' work, to the disgrace of England, and the scorn and amazement of the nations, if the voice of the country do not with one acclaim cry,—'Hold'.

APPENDIX C

Some Absurdities

[*The Crystal Palace and its contents inspired some millions of words of description which mostly ranged from the uncritically adulatory to the downright absurd. One of the best contemporary descriptions was published by J. Tallis and Co., in two volumes edited by J. G. Strutt and profusely illustrated with steel engravings made from daguerreotypes taken of nearly all the exhibits. Tallis's* History *and* Description *praises what is praiseworthy but also exposes the more glaring examples of faulty design, bad taste or vulgar over-decoration of so many exhibits. It is also one of the few contemporary publications to ridicule the ridiculous as the following extracts show:*]

We will accordingly proceed to enumerate a few of the absurdities, which, in amusing variety, were brought before the eyes of the curious and astonished observer in the Crystal Palace.

> 'There are more things in heaven and earth
> Than are dreamt of in your philosophy,
> Horatio',

was the shrewd observation of the sagacious Hamlet, but we feel assured that even his philosophy never indulged in such wild speculations as were put forth in the ever-memorable year of 1851, to an admiring world, in the far-famed precincts of the wondrous House of Glass.

Philosophy in Sport made Science in Earnest, was the title of a little book which we recollect reading with very great pleasure some years ago; and, published at a time when the generality of the community had hardly begun to inquire 'in earnest' into the important secrets of natural and physical science, now every day producing such useful practical results, the modest duodecimo in question did good service by awakening and inviting very many individuals to the pleasure and advantages of various branches of study, which they would otherwise never have dreamed of including within their province of intellectual observation. But 'Philosophy in Sport' is not always 'Science in Earnest', and industry, unguided by the unerring truths of philosophy and the essential demands of utility, is sometimes nothing better than 'industry run mad'. Industry is one thing, and caprice is another and very different thing; in like manner we may say that ingenuity is one thing, and whimsicality another; persevering good sense is one thing, and persevering folly a very different thing: so of workmanship and the production of a useful article, when compared with a prolonged waste of human labour in concocting and finishing a trifle, a toy or an absurdity. These things all involve a different species of effort and result, and call for a very different sort of estimate. Amidst the innumerable examples of well-applied labour in the Great Exhibition, it must, nevertheless, be confessed that there were also a considerable number ... in the construction of which we are bound to say that much thought, and yet more labour, have been most grievously misapplied.

Foremost amongst these we must place Count Dunin's 'Man of Steel', which is an invention of so singular and puzzling a nature, that we feel convinced the author of it must have taken his degree in the academy of Laputa, among the celebrated professors there so admirably described by Swift. Indeed, as respects the utter inutility of his most elaborate production, he has gone far beyond the experimental philosophers of the Flying Island. The worthy experimentalist who ingeniously attempted to extract sunbeams out of cucumbers, had at least some pretence towards a useful purpose; and the learned and literary world would have had reason to bless, had it but succeeded, the projector of the noble idea, far superior to the wonderful calculating machine, from the aid of which 'the most ignorant person, at a reasonable charge, and with little bodily labour, might write books in philosophy, poetry, politics, laws, mathematics, and theology, without the least assistance from genius or study'. We shall not attempt to enter into a description of this most desirable piece of machinery, but we think it might be worth the while of the inventor of the 'great iron man' were he carefully to peruse the whole of the renowned Gulliver's account of the proceedings of these sublime philosophers of Laputa, nothing doubting that he would profit by many of the hints and descriptions he would there find detailed. His piece of mechanism was in the figure of a man, and was constructed of seven thousand pieces of steel. Most of them appeared to be either springs or slides, and they were so put together and arranged as to be capable of a graduated movement, by means of which the proportions of the whole figure might be expanded from the Apollo Belvidere to that of a Goliath. From these colossal proportions it might again be contracted at pleasure to any size between them and its original standard. The mechanism was composed of 875 framing pieces, 48 grooved steel plates, 163 wheels, 202 slides, 476 metal washers, 482 spiral springs, 704 sliding plates, 497 nuts, 5,800 fixing and adjusting screws, with numerous steadying pins, so that the number of pieces was upwards of 7,000. The only utility we ever heard suggested as derivable from this elaborate piece of mechanism, was its applicability to the various measurements of army clothiers or tailors, as it would serve for the figures of men of various sizes. We do not know whether this was the purpose assigned to it by the inventor, as it seems a very absurd one; the same result being far more easily attainable by the incomparably more simple means of half-a-dozen dummies or wooden lay-figures.

But hold! It behoves us to speak with deference and humility in this matter, seeing that the Council of Chairmen of Juries, the supreme heads of wisdom, to whom the dispensation of the Exhibition honours was intrusted, thought proper to reward the constructor of this huge mechanical toy with a 'Council Medal'. Yes, hear it Troughton and Sims, who talk about novelties in scientific instruments, to whom a council medal was denied though recommended by the jury; hear it Claussen, whose newly-discovered and nationally important processes in the preparation of flax received only a common medal; hear it Losely, whose compensating pendulum was one of the most ingenious and valuable improvements in horology in the whole Exhibition —hear it Applegarth, whose vertical printing machine—hear it all ye whose performances had to share the common fate of merit commended 'in a certain degree';—the Jury in Class X awarded, and the Council of Chairmen confirmed to Count E. Dunin a council medal 'For the extraordinary application of mechanism to his expanding figure of a man'. After reading this result, we begin to be somewhat doubtful about all we set out with touching 'philosophy in Sport', and nice distinctions between 'ingenuity' and 'whimsicality' and so forth. . . .

Still in the philosophical instrument department, we come upon 'an apparatus of a peculiar construction, showing the ebb and flow of the tides', exhibited by a Mr Ryles of Cobridge, Staffordshire Potteries, who thus describes the novel theory it is intended to illustrate: 'The article I sent to the Exhibition, is an attempt *to illustrate the idea of the earth being a living creature encased in a shell*, as a snail-house or a sea shell, and by the action of the heart, causing the tide to ebb and flow. Press down the blower, and the heart (as seen through the glass that is on the top of the shell), will contract, causing the tide to rise; let out the air of the shell, and the heart will expand, causing the tide to fall.' He adds, 'I want a patron that would enable me to show how *the tide causes the rotary motion of the earth*, which only poverty prevents my doing.' Mr Ryles has *not* received a Council Medal, nor even 'honourable mention', which, considering the honours heaped upon the 'expanding figure of a man', we consider hard. The least Count Dunin could have done, would have been to have shared his Council Medal with Ryles. . . .

Dr Grey invented and displayed a medical walking-staff, containing instruments [*including an enema syringe*], medicines and other professional articles. Would not a small tin case have answered the same purpose better? ... An 'artificial silver nose' has been invented by Mr Whitehouse. We will not pronounce rashly upon this; but it strikes us that all artificial noses, both in shape, size and the amount of nose required, will depend on the amount wanting by an individual, and the size and shape suited to his particular case. . . .

Mr M'Clintock, of York, exhibited a chain in regular links, the whole of which, we are informed, had been cut out of a solid block of wood; to what purpose, except to the unnecessary length of time such a performance must occupy, we are totally at a loss to conceive. Mr M'Clintock has, however, been surpassed by a lieutenant in the navy, whose name escapes us ... who had achieved the same result from a block of wood, with the help of no other tool but a penknife. Will anybody endeavour to surpass them both, we wonder, by doing the same thing with a pin? ...

'The semibreve guitar' of Mr Dobrowsky was a good thought enough for a new name, and for a fresh attempt to prolong the sound of the notes of the guitar; but if the inventor would have us understand by the term 'Semibreve' that his instrument will sustain a note of any such duration, we must plead absolute scepticism to the possibility of any instrument of this kind being made to accomplish such a result. The enharmonic guitar, manufactured by Panormo, of High Street, Bloomsbury, claims for its original inventor and designer no less a person than Colonel Perronet Thompson, M.P., who some years ago invented a new kind of organ. Of the enharmonic guitar ... it was announced that it was 'capable of being arranged in the perfect ratios for upwards of twenty keys.' We do not doubt this; we accept it at once, not only from what we know of the capabilities of a guitar, but of the scientific attainments of Colonel Thompson; but after his enharmonic guitar has been 'arranged' for any of these keys, what will be the effect of 'playing' in them, amidst all this mechanical interference with the finger-board? ...

An American inventor of the name of Wood, exhibited a combination of the pianoforte and violin, with which he assumes that pieces can be played with the effect of these two instruments in concert ... in the present instance the inventor has literally attached a violin, played upon by four bows, which are put in motion by a separate set of keys on a small upper finger-board, which cause the bows to 'saw' upwards and downwards with an effect which we frankly confess to be indescribable. One might see the whole operation, and a more ludicrous thing, both to see and hear, it has seldom been our lot to experience....

Another inventor exhibited a 'model of a carriage', which supplied its own railway, laying it down as it advanced, and taking it up after the wheels had passed over. This was no doubt extremely ingenious, but unfortunately it *supposed* the existence of a level line for the operation, so that its utility becomes rather questionable....

Principal Sources

BEAVER, PATRICK, *The Crystal Palace*, Hugh Evelyn, London 1970.

BERLYN, PETER & FOWLER, CHARLES, *The Crystal Palace: its Architectural History & Constructional Marvels*, James Gilbert, London 1851.

CHANCE, J. F., *History of Chance Brothers and Company*, privately published, London 1919.

COLE, SIR HENRY, KCB, *Fifty Years of Public Life* (2 vols), George Bell & Sons, London 1884.

DOWNES, CHARLES, *The Building Erected in Hyde Park for the Great Exhibition of the Works of Industry of All Nations* (Fox & Henderson's working drawings and explanatory notes), John Wheale & Co., London 1852.

FAY, C. R., *Palace of Industry, 1851*, Cambridge University Press, Cambridge 1951.

HOBHOUSE, CHRISTOPHER, *1851 and the Crystal Palace*, John Murray, London 1937.

MARKHAM, VIOLET R., CH, *Paxton and the Bachelor Duke*, Hodder & Stoughton, London 1935.

PRIESTLEY, J. B., *Victoria's Heyday*, William Heinemann Ltd, London 1972.

ROLT, L. T. C., *Victorian Engineering*, Allen Lane, London 1970.

TALLIS, JOHN & CO., *Tallis's History and Description of the Crystal Palace and the Exhibition of the World's Industry* (2 vols), John Tallis & Co., London 1852.

VICTORIA AND ALBERT MUSEUM, *The Great Exhibition of 1851*, H.M.S.O., London 1950.

Index

Bessemer-Chance process, 56
Bessemer, Henry, 55, 56
Bessemer process (of steel manufacture), 47, 55
'Big Ben', 33
Birmingham, 11, 41, 54, 55, 56, 126
Biver, Monsieur, 54; *see also* Chance Brothers
blocks, pulley: Brunel's machines for making, 78
Board of Trade, 11, 16, 33
'bone china', 7
Bouch, Thomas, 47, 65
Boulton and Watt, Messrs, 48
Boulton, Matthew, 2
British Association (for the Advancement of Science, f. 1831), 11
British Museum, 132, 140
Brock's fireworks at CP (S), 131
Brougham, Lord, 24, 35-6, 133
Brunel, Isambard Kingdom (engineer and ship-builder), 12, 20-7, 37, 45, 48, 65, 78, 129, 153, 154
Buckland, Sir Henry, 150 *passim*

Canning, Lord, 118
Carlisle, Lord, 123
cat-walks (lead-covered) on CP, 78, 85, 87
Chadwick, Sir Edwin, 8
Chance Brothers and Co., of Birmingham (sheet-glass manufacturers), 41, 50, 54-8 *passim*, 127
Chance, J. F., 57
Chance, Robert Lucas, 41, 55, 56, 63
Chatsworth estate (in Derbyshire), 29-31 *passim*, 34, 35, 38, 86, 121, 122, 129; Great Conservatory and Lily House, 30, 56, 57

Chelsea Waterworks, 79
Chester–Holyhead Railway, 48
Chiswick House, 29, 31
Cobden, Richard, 8, 17
Cockerell, C. R., 20, 37, 153
Cole, Mr (*later* Sir) Henry ('Felix Summerly'), x, 3-4, 10, 39, 118 & *n*, 135; personal details, 4, 5-8, 11; and RSA, 8, 10, 15, 16; and Paris Exposition (1849), 11-12; and RC, 15, 60-1; his propaganda, 15-17; and City of London, 16; and 'revocation' clause, 17; his 'alternative plan' clause, 33, 40; and Fox, Henderson and Chance, 41; and the Press, 60-1; in charge of exhibits, 95-6 *passim*; and painting delays, 95-6; and the sparrows, 98; on the mishap (7 Oct. 1851), 113; his rewards, 118 & *n*; and disposal of funds, 134; and marriage of arts and science, 141; retired, knighted (1875), 141; and South Kensington Museum, 141; and central collections as reservoirs, 141; favoured admission charges, 141-2; opposed Sunday closing, 142; on fire hazards, 144-6; and the penny post, 155 *n*; his *Memoirs* (extracts from, Appendix A), 153-8; his death (1882), 141
colour scheme and decoration of CP, 94-5, 130
columns, the (supporting CP), 42, 47-9 *passim*, 50-2, 68, 69, 71-3, 130; siting of, 51-2; diagonal bracing, *illustrated*, 74; colours on, 94
Commemorative Album (HMSO), 96-7
Commissioners, *see* Royal Commission

wood and iron: alternatives for some parts of CP, 66, 77-8
Woodhead tunnel (through the Pennines): casualties during construction, 63
Woods and Forests, Department of, 11
woodwork in fabric of CP, 43, 62, 66, 78, 80; machining of, 53, 62, 77-9
Wyatt, Matthew Digby, 95